Dedicated to Ian

Trapped in Amber

Trapped in Amber

By

Gordon F Gatiss (Ph.D)

Mind For Life

Trapped in Amber

First published in the UK in May 2011 by
Mind For Life Ltd, The Croft, 9 Hexham Gardens, Moorside,
Consett, Co. Durham. DH8 8LQ
www.mindforlife.co.uk

For bulk or special sales please contact books@mindforlife.co.uk

A catalogue record for this book is available from the British Library.   ISBN 978-0-9568590-0-6

Cover photographs by Bill Phillips.
Cover design by Steven Carruthers and Michael Dunbar.
Printed and bound in the UK by the MPG Books Group, Bodmin and King's Lynn.

Trapped in Amber

Acknowledgements:

I acknowledge that on the course of my journey, many of my choices have affected others. Some of my choices resulted in love and growth, however, in hindsight I can now understand that some were unnecessary, and caused pain. I did not know then what I know now; I ask for you not to live in memory of what I was, but in what I am, and will become.

I thank my brother Nigel for his honesty, wisdom and wonderful poetry.

To Rob Lindsay, who thought he was in the wrong place, but it turned out that he was in the right place. Thank you for sharing your time on your journey enriching my experience. The Universe knows who you are.

To David Corr for his advice and support.

Trapped in Amber

Trapped in Amber

Synopsis:

A book for the person who is serious about enhancing and changing their life; written by a Psychotherapist from personal experience, and of working with many people. The narrative explains a radical proven way of making beneficial changes in your life. The processes and techniques explained are the results of working with clients since 2002. Hard empirical data has been collected since 2008, showing that clients, who fully participated in the programme, significantly improved their well-being and health in weeks, not months. The narrative is thought provoking, challenging and different, but the words are supported with sound reason and explanation. This is a 'how to book' for those who are serious about finding the desire within to change their life; it will provide the know-how, and understanding behind the process of change that has rarely been explained before in one edition; empowering the reader with knowledge and possibilities.

It is my desire that readers find the narrative challenging, controversial, and thought provoking, causing conflict with their current belief system. If this is the result of reading this book for the first time, then I hope you will read it again, for on further readings, the challenges will become points of interest, which will become knowledge. It is only with knowledge that you can make meaningful changes to your life. Knowledge is not an opinion, it is a practice, that empowers choice and responsibility.

Trapped in Amber

Destiny

Why do we value material wealth,
More than we value mental health?
Why do we value the advent of speed
Over the value of growing the seed?

Why do circumstance and event,
Affect our mood and behavioural intent?
Why allow our life's course
To be controlled by an outside force?

Only I can raise my arm ...
With thought internal anger or calm.
When I live for others to control,
I disempower my being and soul.

Can I be sure my thoughts are real?
My behaviour determined by the deal.
What could be, to change my mind?
That single act could save mankind.

To grow the rose, we plant the seed.
I plant my thoughts to grow my greed.
What I allow determines my life.
Without responsibility I walk in strife.

What changes everything is not without;
What changes everything is within.
Illusion is the world I see,
What I create for me will be.

The force inside shapes the trait;
Regret, doubt, fear insecurity and hate.
How did they get there? Not by circumstance or event,
We put them there with purposeful intent.

This is my life, my time to be.
Whatever I desire of me. It is within;
I have the key,
To shape my own destiny.

Gordon

Trapped in Amber

Trapped in Amber

Introduction:

You only need to read this book if you are serious about making significant enhancement and changes in your life. Why this book? There are many books written about how to free your soul, feed your soul, free your mind, love your planet; there are books about healing, about the Universe, Heaven, Angels, Eastern philosophy, Orbs, and the Moon. This book is none of those. This book is a serious narrative explaining how the mind and body connection works, how to control your mind and body, and how everyone of us is responsible for our own well-being and life.

The narrative is full of techniques to facilitate change. Another difference in this book is that the techniques are supported with the best guess or understanding that science and philosophy has given us, up to the present time, as to the reason why the techniques work. There is no woo woo or magic implied, and therefore the text does explain the implications of cells, brain and other body function in some detail, because the author is committed to enabling the reader not to believe anything written in the book, but to know it. Know(ledge) is the enabler of self-responsibility, belief and faith disempowers through rules, insecurity, and control. The biology of how cells have developed, and how the brain has evolved with the mind, to create a record and recall process of memory, is explained. It is of importance that the narrative is carefully read as the science supports the techniques of change discussed.

The only way you will know that the knowledge shared in this book works for everyone, every time, all the time, is to try it; without pre-judgment. Learn how to release yourself from the boundaries of your belief system.

This book has been created to make you challenge your belief system. It will push buttons that will invoke emotions, and values, providing clear evidence that you are creating an illusion and living in that illusion. The book is written in a clear and blunt style; it does not set out to tell you what to do. It provides a narrative that should enable and empower you, the reader to make up your own mind. Please remember this is only a book of words ... it is not inferring right or wrong, good or bad; it is asking searching questions, and bringing together the best guess or understanding of certain knowledge, in order for you to know. What you do with this knowledge is entirely up to you.

Readers should be prepared to read the narrative knowing that it may not agree with their current perceptions or understanding. The interpretations of the scientific data are my personal best guess or understanding of how the data influences the human life-form. My interpretation of the data has provided new challenging concepts of how we actually interface with our environment.

... be aware of your emotions while
reading the narrative ...

Trapped in Amber

Contents

Trapped in Amber

Trapped in Amber

WHAT IS TRUTH? CAN WE EVER KNOW?

Please read the narrative in this book with the understanding that the knowledge shared, is only the very best guess or understanding that science and philosophy have, at this moment in our time. It is not cast-in-stone … it is only that, which we can either understand or experience, at this moment in our evolution.

It is not presented as TRUTH, which will not or cannot change … it is presented as a snap shot, at this moment in time, for the purpose of enlightenment and healing, with the clear understanding that we will learn more tomorrow, as we build upon what we know today.

Remember we are all on a journey … the narrative is a signpost on that journey. It does not attempt to give answers it only asks questions, some uncomfortable, some will provoke inner searching, others perhaps will amuse. It does however, attempt to make you challenge who you are, and come to your own conclusions about this wonderful adventure called life. All I ask is that you read the narrative trying the exercises and techniques. Do not prejudge, practice the techniques for three months, after which, if you want, you can revert back to your old way of living, nothing lost; or uncover a wonderful way to live your life.

Trapped in Amber

Trapped in Amber

Be aware of your emotions while reading the narrative.

CAN YOU BE ABSOLUTELY SURE THAT WHAT YOU BELIEVE IS TRUE?

The key words in the question are 'absolutely sure' ... because most people only believe things they are prepared to accept. But can you be absolutely sure, I mean *absolutely sure*, that even the things you are sure you are sure about, are absolutely true? True in the sense that they are irrefutable, they can be proved to be true under rigorous testing; the results are always the same, every time all the time and will never change. Or do some of your beliefs fall under the headings of; tradition (religious or otherwise), manners, culture, always done it that way, that is what I was taught, everyone does it; I saw it on the television or read it in a newspaper. So it always happens this/that way. Then we may have other beliefs, examples like; they are a different religion, they are a different colour, implying that religion or colour, labels the way people think, and it must be different from the way you think.

Let me drill down to the crux of the question; consider the personal things you believe to be true. I'm too fat ... she doesn't love me ... I can't do that ... I'm not good enough, blame, guilt, fear, fault; these may be some of your daily thought patterns.

Are your personal beliefs a comparison to a standard that your belief system indicates is relevant? Note here that your belief system is setting the standard and doing the comparison. It's like setting your own exam questions, and then marking them. You will always get what you have always got because you only set questions you think you can answer, so you always give the same answers, getting the same results. Strange as this may sound, even though you set the questions, do you often get the answers wrong? Why? ... Perhaps you are trying to change your life using the same mind that gave you the problem. The mind (belief system) that gives you a problem cannot give you the solution; it can only give you what it already has. Could it be that to change your life you need to change your mind ... you need to change your belief system?

... nothing divides as much as belief ...

Trapped in Amber

Be aware of your emotions while reading the narrative.

DO YOU ACCEPT THAT WHAT YOU BELIEVE AFFECTS YOUR BEHAVIOUR?

Your behaviour is totally driven by what you believe. You will do something or not do something, totally dependent on your belief system. If you procrastinate or keep changing your mind, it is because your belief system is wired to make you 'behave' in such a manner. Generally you will not do something that your belief system considers inappropriate. It is possible that you can make a choice that is counter intuitive to your belief system; however, if this is done without purpose, such action usually causes stress or anxiety.

When a person has a strong belief about a situation, and uses that belief to persuade others, then this is often labeled a 'faith', which relies on rules and conformity with punishments and consequences. It is different strong belief systems that create conflict and division, limiting the ability of the holders to a fixed view. Could it be that you will always believe what you believe, because if you accepted that there may be another (possibly better) way, that might have an effect on how you, perceive other people, perceive you. Do you live your life concerned or worrying how other people perceive you?

Consider this situation.

Some years ago a female client, in her forties, came to see me. I will call her Susan (not her real name). She told me that when she had been a young girl, fourteen years of age, she had been bullied at school. Her journey home from school took her through a small park which overlooked her house. She often stopped in the park, sitting on a seat next to a small pond. This day a cat jumped up onto the seat beside her. She started to stroke the cat and talk to it, telling it all about the girl who was bullying her at school. After a short while she went home, and after her tea, she spent the rest of the evening in her bedroom, worrying about school the next day. She had been unable to tell her parents anything about the problems she was having.

The next day the girl who was bullying her did not arrive at school; Susan later found out that she had left the school because her family was moving to another town. On her way home that evening Susan stopped off at her usual place in the park, and to her surprise the same cat came and sat down beside her. Susan actually remembers this event very well; as she told me she actually thanked the cat for sorting out her problem. She does not know why she thanked the cat, Susan just explained that it felt the right thing to do.

Ever since that day Susan has talked to cats about her problems, and she believes that all her issues have been sorted out because of this. Even coming to see me had been what she called a serendipitous moment. She now has her own cats, and apparently while she had been surfing the internet at random, with her two cats sitting next to her, my website had appeared. She had relationship issues, and was also unhappy in her current work role; her cats were obviously aware of this as she had confided in them. So she made the decision that my website was a sign, and she made an appointment to come and see me to talk over what she could do.

Now is there any proof that talking to cats in anyway has any effect on resolving people's problems? If Susan had chosen to pray to a Divine God about her problems, and as was the case, most were resolved; would that be proof that a God had any effect on the person's problems?

Trapped in Amber

Trapped in Amber

Be aware of your emotions while reading the narrative.

WHAT COULD YOU BE WITHOUT YOUR CURRENT BELIEF SYSTEM?

Would you accept that your belief system limits your ability to those things your belief system determines is true? What is truth? Is it a fundamental law, is it a formula, is it something handed down from generation to generation? If it is not truth for all life on Earth for always, then perhaps it is not truth; perhaps it is only the best guess or understanding at that moment in time for a certain number of people? Could it be that 'belief' is an illusion that allows life to make sense of the environment? If you can convince enough people to believe your truth then you have power and control; it is still not the truth, it is still only your illusion. The cat is still only a cat?

I will now attempt to explain some amazing insights that are currently accepted as the best guess or understanding science has at this moment. Then I will take you through the steps that will show you how to change your current belief system and change your life. This is possibly not the only way to do this, but it is the way that I personally have changed my life; so it is something that I have experience of, and can affirm, and know has worked for me, and I have taught it with equal success to many clients since 2004. So I do not want you to believe it, or have faith that it will work, I want you to know it. I am going to describe the process, and if you want to try it for yourself you can ... if not then you can also do that.

There is no magic, no need for a faith or intervention of a Divinity or God-like entity. The narrative will show you how to take responsibility for your life. I will not do anything, you will do it all; you will make all the decisions, all the choices; you will choose your life.

To start a journey it is often wise to have a destination in mind, so that when you get there you know you are there. However, the journey of life is different for it has no destination ... you do not stop living while you are living ... life is the journey. So do not have a preconceived idea of what your life will be, because it can change in an instant. Circumstances outside your control may change your life, but your response to those circumstances will determine what that life achieves; your response 'your journey of life', is all your responsibility and within your control. The journey of life will always be about evolution; *your* evolution. Your development, to each successive stage or part of your life is moving towards the end of our physical cellular life; death and the release of the life-force from within.

... you do not stop living while you
are living, life is the journey ...

Trapped in Amber

—

Be aware of your emotions while reading the narrative.

HOW DO YOU MEASURE YOUR LIFE ON PLANET EARTH?

Do you measure it in a hard form that can be seen and touched like financial and material wealth? Do you see people with financial and material wealth as successful? Is that how you will measure your life?

Do you measure it in a soft form like happiness, love, family, and friends?

Is your perception that life is hard and difficult and full of compromises?

Is your measure of life a combination of hard and soft options?

Your perceptions will determine how you journey through life, but the end result will always be the same; death of the physical body and release of the life-force within. Now you could be excused for asking the obvious question, "What is the purpose of life?" Is life just the means to death, and once we die is that it? If that is correct then does it not suggest that life therefore has no meaning, so just enjoy it while you can, and take as much as you can while you can, because in the end it does not matter? Could that have been why Gods were invented to try and control people, with a promise that after death there will be a better place for those who are compliant?

Or perhaps life has a deeper purpose? It is just as easy to believe in the '*after death there is nothing argument*', as it is to believe in a '*God Entity argument*'. However, it is as easy to believe in a different view of the purpose of life. Perhaps Planet Earth is a school where life is given the opportunity to learn how to create, through intention, a unified and equal form of being, in preparation for the next part of the journey, *being* without the physical body?

It would be remiss of me to simply tell you about the techniques and processes involved in helping you to change your life, and not explain why it is that those techniques and processes work. The explanation is the best guess or understanding that we have at this moment, and involves a brief bit of 'science'. Now I am aware that some readers may find the following few pages challenging, and they may wonder why the information is necessary. My answer is simple ... I do not want you *to believe* that the techniques and processes in this book will help you to change your life ... *I desire that you know*. The only way that I know they work is because I follow them. However, it is because I have spent many years researching why I did, and thought certain things, that I came to understand, and know how my mind and body are connected. It is because I desired to have that understanding that I acknowledge my responsibility to demonstrate the educational journey that occurred in me when I discovered this knowledge.

I have tried to keep the technical 'stuff' simple, and I politely ask that you try and persist with reading the narrative so that you can gain some understanding of who you really are. I am not saying it is the truth or that you definitely need to understand, however, please accept that it's possible that it is important, in that it will briefly explain the understanding that scientists have at this moment, about how your mind and body works. Stick with it, and perhaps you will learn something you didn't know. Only with new knowledge is it possible to change your perception. The science is explained in an attempt to help you to understand how fantastic you are, and that you do not work by magic; you do not have to remember the detail, simply appreciate you are a product of evolution and you are still evolving.

To explain in more detail let me ask the question; "What is your body?" "What happens to your body when you die?" Our understanding at this moment is that when we die our physical bodies go back to the natural state of atoms. Your body is made up of eleven primary atoms, they are; Hydrogen 10%, Carbon 20%, Oxygen 60%. Then 9% of your body is made from Nitrogen, Phosphorus and Calcium; about 0.9% of your body is made from Chlorine, Potassium, Sodium, Magnesium and Sulphur, the remaining 0.1% consists of other trace elements including a small amount of gold. Scientific knowledge at this moment identifies that an atom consists of a nucleus, which consists of protons and neutrons; the nucleus is called 'matter' or 'mass'.

The nucleus, consisting of protons and neutrons, is in the centre of the atom, while the electrons orbit the outside diameter. The electrons do not 'orbit' in the sense that they go around and around the atom, the electrons are potential electrons; they appear in different places around the atom without actually going in the space between appearances. If you lay one million atoms in a line next to each other they would be approximately the thickness of one strand of hair from your head. The ratio of nucleus to the size of the atom is equivalent to imagining electrons orbiting a sphere in Space, twenty miles in diameter, forming a ball-like structure. In the centre of the twenty mile ball-like structure in Space, is a piece of matter (the nucleus) the size of a football. That is the approximate scale of the nucleus to the size of an atom. An atom is 99.99% vacuum, in other words there is nothing between the nucleus and the cloud of electrons. It is the strong nuclear force that binds the protons and neutrons to each other in the nucleus. The current understanding is that if you take the vacuum in a single hydrogen atom, the latent energy in that vacuum holds a trillion times more energy than the mass of all the stars, and all of the planets within twenty billion light years from Planet Earth. (Tiller, W.A. 1997, 2001) The human body consists of 10% hydrogen atoms.

The atoms that our bodies are made from could not have been made on Planet Earth; they could only be formed in the heat and pressure of the forming and destruction of stars. The atoms that we are made from were made in the Stars in the Universe. We are Stardust. We are part of the fabric of the Universe, we are children of the Universe, and all things on Planet Earth are made from the same atoms. Every rock, pebble, grain of sand, tree, plant, ant, elephant, bird, dog, cat, and human. All life-forms are made from atoms that were made in the Universe. Atoms make cells. All things made of atoms have the potential of unimaginable energy bound in the nucleus, they cannot be anything else. This includes you.

There are two primary types of cell; a prokaryotic cell and an eukaryotic cell. The two cell types have a lot in common. They perform most of the same kinds of functions, and in the same ways. Both are enclosed by plasma membranes, filled with cytoplasm, and loaded with small structures called ribosomes. Both have DNA which carries the instructions for operating the cell. And the similarities go far beyond the visible; physiologically they are very similar in many ways. For example, the DNA in the two cell types is precisely the same kind of DNA, and the genetic code for a prokaryotic cell is exactly the same genetic code used in eukaryotic cells. A eukaryotic cell is bigger and more complex than a prokaryotic cell.

Brief summary of a prokaryotic cell:

★   It is smaller than an eukaryotic cell, and all materials within the cell are relatively close together.

★   They have no nucleus.

★   They do posses DNA (deoxyribonucleic acid) and DNA functions.

★   The DNA is circular; it has no ends. It has one main DNA molecule and a varied assortment of smaller circlets of DNA called 'plasmids'.

★   DNA is naked in that it has no 'histones' associated with it, and it is not formed into chromosomes.

★   The centre of the cell is known as the 'nucleoid' because it is approximately where the DNA is located.

The 'nucleoid' is an imaginary structure as there is no boundary enclosing it.

★ It has fewer genes than a eukaryotic cell.

★ Contains no membrane-bound organelles which are independent of the plasma membrane. This is a significant difference between the two cell types.

★ Cell division is by binary fission, and reproduction is always asexual.

Brief summary of an eukaryotic cell.

★ Larger than a prokaryotic cell.

★ The cell has a true nucleus bound by a double membrane. The purpose of the nucleus is to sequester the DNA related functions of the big cell into a smaller chamber, for the purpose of increased efficiency.

★ The DNA (deoxyribonucleic acid) is linear.

★ The DNA is complex with proteins called 'histones', and is organized into a number of chromosomes.

★ The inside (cytoplasm) is filled with a large complex collection of organelles, (cells within a cell that perform the function of an organ); many of the organelles are enclosed in their own membrane increasing the efficiency of the functions confined within.

★ More space inside the cell than in a prokaryotic cell.

★ Cell division is by mitosis or meiosis, and reproduction is asexual or sexual.

Mitosis and meiosis are two types of cell division. Mitosis is cell division that results in the duplication of cells; the daughter cells are genetic copies of the parent cell. This cell multiplication allows for replacement of old cells, tissue repair, growth and development. Mitosis is the process that enabled you to grow and develop in the womb to become you.

As an important component in the process of sexual reproduction, meiosis is the means by which one cell divides into four different cells. Meiosis takes its name from the Greek word meioun, which translated means to make something smaller. In effect, that is what happens when meiosis occurs in the human life-form. A diploid eukaryotic cell (a cell with forty six chromosomes) will begin a process of dividing into four more or less equal portions, referred to as haploid cells. The number of chromosomes contained in each of the haploid cells, created from the diploid cell, is reduced to twenty three. Chromosomes contain the basic DNA chain that will determine the physical characteristics of the child in the event that a pregnancy takes place.

During the process of meiosis, the genome of the diploids begins to undergo two distinct rounds of division that ultimately result in the four haploid cells. Each of the haploid cells or gametes will contain one fully complete strand of chromosomes, (twenty three) which equates to half of the chromosomes supplied by the previous division. The gametes are capable of meshing or fusing with other opposite gender haploid cells during the process of fertilization.

If the fertilization is successful, this leads to the creation of a zygote, (forty six chromosomes). This is important to note, as the union of these two different gender diploids contain the DNA strands of both of the haploid cells, resulting in a unique physiological makeup of a new life. In other words, in the human life-form, the male sperm is a haploid cell containing twenty three chromosomes; the female egg is a haploid cell, also containing a different but complementary set of twenty three chromosomes. When they fertilize the chromosomes join together to form new cells with forty six chromosomes.

The need for two haploid cells to form the zygote is one of the characteristics that set the process of meiosis apart from other means of reproduction, such as mitosis. While both meiosis and mitosis will rely on some of the same mechanisms to aid in chromatin distribution, it is important to remember that mitosis occurs as a form of asexual reproduction, meaning there is no need for a combination of opposite gender gametes, which is only a non-sexual form of reproduction. Chromatin is the mass of genetic material composed of DNA and proteins that condense to form chromosomes during eukaryotic cell division; chromatin is located in the nucleus of a cell. Meiosis results in genetic variations that are based on the unique composition of the two opposite gametes, rather than the creation of new life from a single source.

The two cells are more alike than different, and scientists at this moment are convinced that the cells are evolutionary linked. The eukaryotic cell evolved from the prokaryotic cell, because during the first 3.8 billion years, life on Planet Earth only consisted of single-celled organisms like bacteria, algae, and yeast, (prokaryotic cells). Then around seven hundred million years ago cells started to evolve into primitive multi-cellular organisms.

So to summarize there are two distinct types of cell; prokaryotic and eukaryotic. Prokaryotic cells differ from eukaryotic cells in that they do not have a membrane-bound nucleus. Prokaryotic cells can form colonial forms of organism with limited organizational ability, but they either survive independently or within a colonial 'life-form' organism. A prokaryotic cell will die if taken out of a colonial organism. Eukaryotic cells have a distinct membrane bound nucleus where chromosomal DNA is found.

Chromosomes vary in number and shape among living forms. Most bacteria have one or two circular chromosomes. Humans, along with other animals and plants, have linear chromosomes that are arranged in pairs within the nucleus of the cell. The only human cells that do not contain pairs of chromosomes are reproductive cells, or gametes, which carry just one copy of each chromosome. When two reproductive cells unite, they become a single cell that contains ████ copies of each chromosome. This cell then divides and its successors divide numerous times, eventually producing a mature individual with a full set of paired chromosomes in virtually all of its cells.

Besides the linear chromosomes found in the nucleus, the cells of humans and other complex organisms carry a much smaller type of chromosome similar to those seen in bacteria. This circular chromosome is found in mitochondria, which are structures located outside the nucleus that serve as the cell's powerhouses.

Scientists think that, in the past, mitochondria were free-living bacteria with the ability to convert oxygen into energy. When these bacteria invaded cells lacking the power to tap into oxygen's power, the cells retained them, and, over time, the bacteria evolved into modern-day mitochondria.

Eukaryotic cells can form multi-cellular organisms, and operate as one organism with complex organizational intelligence, and each cell can exist outside the organism. Humans are a eukaryotic multi-celled entity.

Trapped in Amber

Trapped in Amber

Be aware of your emotions while reading the narrative.

HOW DOES THIS HAVE ANY BEARING ON YOUR LIFE?

A woman 1.7 meters tall, weighing sixty one kilos would have approximately sixty trillion eukaryotic cells making up her body. Current research suggests that there are over two hundred and twenty different types of eukaryotic cell in the human body. Many cells having specific functions and structure; example nerve cells are electrically excitable. Muscle cells are long and slender containing fibers that help in relaxing and contracting action of the muscles. Among the many other types of cell there are skin cells, fat cells, sex cells, heart cells, and liver cells.

Interestingly the red blood cells are eukaryotic cells that have lost their nucleus and are known as erythrocytes. The blood consists of a suspension of special cells in a liquid called *'plasma'*. In an adult man, the blood is about eight percent of the body weight; about five to six litres. Blood consists of 55% *plasma*, and 45% by cells called *'formed elements.'* There is no DNA in a red blood cell, plasma or platelet. DNA is only present in white blood cells.

Blood is separated by the Blood Service into three main components; red blood cells, plasma and platelets, the white blood cell is filtered and destroyed. Red blood cells would be used in a transfusion to replace major blood loss, and or to treat a medical condition (no DNA). Platelets would be used when people have low platelet counts; for example when people have leukaemia, or when people have had high doses of chemotherapy, or when people have had a bone marrow transplant (no DNA). Plasma is the fluid in the blood that contains clotting proteins, and is given to patients after lots of blood transfusions, or to people with conditions such as liver disease (no DNA).

The reason why we can receive blood from some people and not others is due to the antigens (on the cell surface) and the antibodies in the plasma. Of course, these are genetically determined, but as there are around twenty blood types this means that it is not the actual individual's genome that determines whether they can receive blood, but is due to only a few genes that code for antigens/antibodies. Perhaps it may also have something to do with having no DNA?

White blood cells have DNA, and are one of the cells the body makes to fight infection. There are several types of white blood cell and they are known as leukocytes. The white blood cells have a short life cycle, living only for a few days to a few weeks. A drop of blood can contain between seven thousand to twenty five thousand white blood cells at a time. Too many white blood cells is a symptom of Leukemia, too few and there is a serious risk of bacterial infection often referred to as neutropenia.

All eukaryotic cells are covered with 'spikes' called *receptors,* there could be over one thousand receptors on one cell. These receptors are the guardians of the cell; nothing can enter or leave the cell unless it can match to a receptor. Anything that enters the cell changes the behaviour of the cell. A eukaryotic cell is a cell with a nucleus where DNA resides. There is approximately fifteen billion miles of DNA in the average human adult. That is enough DNA to stretch to the moon and back over thirty thousand times; or stretch to the sun and back over seventy times.

Eukaryotic cells exist in all animals, plants, fungi and protists, which are organisms that include amoebae, red algae and slime mould. The atoms in the human body will be replaced with a new atom every twelve to eighteen months. The atoms in your body now could have been in a dinosaur, a tree, an ant or an elephant. We are physically changing all the time as we are constantly recycled.

Based on the established scientific view as to what our bodies are, we can look deeper into the current research to identify that the atoms we are made from, somehow make molecules, which form eukaryotic cells. These cells form groups and make organs, which link together to create whole or complete/distinct life-forms. How atoms, molecules and cells know what life-form to create is still a mystery to us at this moment. Theory suggests that all living entities have an electromagnetic field, sometimes referred to as the morphogenetic field, and cells are influenced by the morphic resonance of the parent to produce off-spring with the same resonance. In developmental biology, a morphogenetic field is a group of cells that are able to respond to localized biochemical signals leading to the development of like for like, specific morphogenetic structures.

Example, cells in a limb morphogenetic field will become limb tissue; those in a heart field will become heart tissue. Your arms and legs have exactly the same chemicals and cells, including the same DNA in the cells, yet they are different. Rupert Sheldrake likened the morphogenetic field to an architectural plan of a building. He suggested that you could build different shaped buildings using exactly the same materials; the differences would be a result of the architectural plans. The morphogenetic field is the architectural plans of the cell that puts *'information'* into the cell to give it form, (puts form into the *life*-form). There is also evidence that off-spring are similar to parent(s) due to DNA and cell membrane receptors.

It is accepted that we have a field of energy, flowing around our bodies. This field is created by the electrical energy produced by our heart, and the electrochemical actions of our cells. This energy can be measured, and research is ongoing to understand the implications of this energy on the health and well-being for human life. The well established and old Japanese healing technique of Reiki uses the body's energy field as a source of healing. This energy field is often referred to as the Body Aura.

The body's energy fields are different depending upon your health, stress levels, frame of mind, and general well-being. Understanding them and learning how to manipulate and work with them, can enhance your health significantly.

I am here, NOW, in a human form,
on Planet Earth.

Keep repeating the last phrase over and over to yourself. As the days pass you may find yourself asking questions that you have never asked before. Questions like: *What is a thought? What is an emotion?*

How many times a day do you think? It would seem that the actual process of *thinking* is an ongoing activity that is done automatically in many instances, but can be provoked, and under specific circumstances can be overwhelming and consuming.

Trapped in Amber

Be aware of your emotions while reading the narrative.

HOW HAVE WE DEVELOPED THE ABILITY TO THINK?

The more knowledge we have of who we are, and how our mind and body work, the better understanding we will have of how easy it is to change our behaviour. So to answer the question, it is possible, that we need to understand more of the scientific and biological research that's been done, relating to the human life-form.

Scientific theory is that a brain-type function evolved within the cell. Theory suggests that in the beginning a simple prokaryotic cell had consciousness and a simple brain function. This evolved into an eukaryotic cell, which evolved a more complex brain to survive in a more complex environment; a form of intelligent operating system, but it did not have the ability to store events as a memory. These simple organisms approached every event in the external environment as new, and were stimulated each time to respond in one way, all the time, every time. Hold the question of what is consciousness, we will discuss that later.

As the external environment became more complex the brain-like function evolved, becoming more complex, adapting to its environment, acquiring new skills. This is a simple theory of how this happened. A single celled eukaryotic entity has an operating system that interprets the external environmental signals, allowing the cell to function. Functions like eating, excreting waste, moving towards food, and moving away from poisons or threats. In other words survival functions, which are encoded in the DNA of the cell. This is achieved with a primitive form of the functions of a brain.

As time passed the external environment became more complex; single eukaryotic cells evolved to join with other eukaryotic cells and became multi-cellular organisms. This action had an advantage as a survival strategy. The primitive brain therefore had to adapt to multi-cellular life evolving more complex functions. So some cells specialized in specific functions within the multi-celled organism, becoming specialists at functioning either as a brain or digestive system or another system of the cell. This is similar to sub routines in a complex software programme for an operating system.

As the brain evolved it developed the ability for the organism to retain the behaviour created from an external signal. It did this by creating an instruction in the form of a chemical to match the external environmental signal;

equipping this chemical with an appropriate switch, allowing it to bind with a receptor on the other cells within the organism. Once this *environmentally-created-chemical-instruction* was infused into other cells, this changed the behaviour of the cell to match the instruction. This also allowed the cells to hold onto the chemical as a reminder of what to do if the same instruction was received again. Whatever affects the behaviour of the cell, can affect the behaviour of the organism. This retention of behaviour connected with external environmental signals has come to be known as memory.

Current understanding (Pert, C. 1997) suggests it works like this; When the multi-cellular eukaryotic organism receives a signal from the external environment then the hypothalamus, a part of the primitive brain responsible for 'flight or fight' instincts and emotions, produces a chemical. This chemical is taken up by the cells within the organism and they either. (1) Respond to the chemical because they have the behaviour memory (chemical) already stored. (2) Or if it is a new chemical, it will have been derived from a thought and emotion. (Note an emotion can be a feeling, a meaning or label attached to a thought.) The DNA in the cell instructs the chemical what to do, and the chemical informs the cell how to behave, and that behaviour is stored for the next time as a chemical marker. Bruce Lipton (2009) suggests that the brain of the eukaryotic cell is the membrane, the equivalent of the cell's skin. Built into the membrane are protein switches that respond to environmental signals.

This chemical produced by the brain to match the external environmental signal is called a peptide. A peptide is a chemical amino acid protein. When this peptide is produced it is chemically and biologically linked to the action(s) and emotion(s) carried out by the organism, and associated thereafter with that action or behaviour. So an external signal from the environment can trigger the organism to take an action, thus causing the organism to behave in a certain way, without the organism having to use up additional time and resource(s).

The human brain is able to perform this feat because it has evolved a process we call the 'mind'. The brain splits this process into two parts, the conscious-mind (not to be confused with consciousness/awareness) and the sub-conscious-mind. The Mind is not a 'thing' it is a process. Breathing is a process, feeling hungry or thirsty is a process within the body. Theory suggests that originally, organisms operated in the conscious-mind. That is in the NOW. Everything was new all the time, and the organism had to make decisions all the time from the signals coming in from its environment. This process was very challenging, and wasteful as a survival strategy. So over billions of years the organism evolved the brain to split the 'mind process' in two, and create a process to store learned patterns of behaviour. This store of learned patterns of behaviour has come to be known as the sub-conscious.

The conscious-mind is *NOW*; the sub-conscious-mind is *BEFORE NOW*, (everything that has happened before the present moment or before THE NOW). The sub-conscious-mind is composed of memory, and repeated memory becomes behaviour. If the *NOW* event is traumatic then the memory imprint is generated with strong concentrated peptide chemicals, and they can become behaviour without going through a repeated memory stage. Humans have taken this phenomena of *NOW* and *BEFORE NOW* (the past) and used logic that implies, if there is a *NOW* and a *BEFORE NOW*, then can there be a future? Perhaps the *FUTURE* is a concept made up by human beings, as a consequence of our minds evolving the ability to separate *NOW* and the *BEFORE NOW*.

The future in relation to the Universe is already set; we cannot stop the Universe from doing anything. We cannot stop the sun from eventually burning out; eternity is not measurable. Planet Earth life is a potential only, because our time frame is something we measure, and therefore it is within the period of eternity, so it is a local future only. By conceiving a concept we call 'future' we have habitually developed strategies, to try and control this concept in our mind, that we call 'future'. The ability to influence local future events (local to the life-form) is a powerful survival advantage, and was arguably one of the most important evolutionary traits in the development of the human race. Many other life-forms have the ability to perceive a future, it is not only a human trait.

Do you realise the implications of having a memory and repeatable behaviour? The implications are that thoughts are a product of environmental signals, utilized by the senses, then observed, received and processed by the brain. (See pages 146/147) That means a thought is *not* real, it is only an *interpretation* of environmental signals. Environmental signals are not interpreted the same way by all living things, therefore a thought is only the interpretation of the life-form; and the life-form can only interpret the signals based on its belief system. Thoughts are not real, they only have meaning or value to the life-form that thinks the thought.

Why is this information important? It is important because we humans are evolved multi-cellular eukaryotic organisms that work exactly as described above. We have a conscious-mind that processes environmental signals in the present moment, the NOW. Environmental signals can come from either the external or internal environment. The conscious-mind is only influenced by your senses. What are your senses? This list is not comprehensive, but is an indication of how sensitive a being you are. Michael J Cohen (2007) lists fifty three senses.

Trapped in Amber

(Int) = Internally Triggered　　　(Ex) Externally triggered

Senses	Example
Equilibrioception (Internal)	Perception of balance
Hearing (External)	Audition
Nociception (Internal)	Perception of pain
Proprioception (Internal)	Perception of body awareness
Psychosomatic (Internal)	Sense of self, friendships, relationships, psychic power
Sense of air/wind pressure (External)	
Sense of body functions (Internal)	Bladder, bowel, sleep, not feeling well
Sense of chemicals (Internal/External)	Hunger, thirst, air, hormones
Sense of colour (External)	
Sense of gravity (External)	
Sense of mood (Internal)	
Sense of motion (Internal/External)	
Sense of temperature (Internal/External)	
Sight (External)	Vision
Smell (External)	Olfaction
Taste (Int/External)	Gustation
Thermoception (External)	Sense of heat
Touch (External)	

The brain monitors your environment all the time, and when a signal is received into your conscious-mind, the brain checks with your sub-conscious to see if the incoming signal, or anything like, it has been received before.

The human brain basically speaking consists of three brains that have emerged through the course of our evolution.
1.. In the centre there is the reptilian brain (developed from the original amphibian brain). This is the oldest of the three controlling vital functions such as heart rate, breathing, body temperature and balance.

2.. Wrapped around this is the Limbic brain, which emerged in the first mammals. It is understood that this 'brain' developed memories and behaviour based on environmental signals. The main structures of the limbic brain are the hippocampus, the amygdala, and the hypothalamus. This 'brain' is the seat or place where we make judgements, which we often make unconsciously, that ultimately affect our behaviour.

3.. The third 'brain' that has evolved, and wraps around the other two, is the neocortex. This brain is responsible among other things for language, and imagination.

The three parts of the brain do not operate independently of one another. They have established interconnections through which they influence one another.

In the human life-form, the current understanding is that the conscious-mind can process information (signals) at about forty nerve impulses per second, while the sub-conscious-mind can process information (signals) at forty million nerve impulses per second. This implies that the sub-conscious-mind is one million times more powerful than the conscious-mind.

If your sub-conscious recognizes the environmental signal, it authorises the hypothalamus, located in your brain, which is responsible for all the autonomic processes in the body, to produce the stored memory peptide. The hypothalamus, with the help of the pituitary gland, floods your blood system with the peptides; resulting in your cells triggering the behaviour you taught it, sometime in the past. (See pages 146/147) If the signal is new, then the brain communicates with the conscious-mind, and the hypothalamus is passed the 'thought' with its attached emotion, meaning or value from the conscious-mind. This is an instruction to the hypothalamus to make a peptide to match this *thought instruction*, which then infuses many cells of the body, obliging the body to respond (behave) in the way instructed. The hypothalamus can produce over one hundred thousand different peptides; this chemical message is uniquely chemically imprinted with the action and emotion you attach to the thought.

A peptide that is accepted by a cell is a message to the cell instructing it how to behave; this will include an emotional state and an action. This communication is instant. It is going on all the time, and has no judgement. Your body will not challenge the instruction from a peptide. The body will not judge the behaviour instructed, it will carry out the instruction exactly. The sub-conscious-mind is a process that has evolved to protect you; it is essential for survival, has no judgement, and has given eukaryotic cell life a competitive advantage.

It is important to realise that we have evolved from cells, and we are still evolving. Evolution has not stopped ... evolution is forever. We are changing; it is just that evolutionary changes happen slowly in terms of the human-time frame. Time is only a concept that we have adopted to give us a means to make sense of the changes we experience. Due to the way our brains continually process environmental signals, which affect our thought patterns, and consequently our behaviour, we have, to a large extent made ourselves prisoners of another human made concept, namely time. We measure changes in periods of seconds, hours, days, weeks, months, years, or events like summer, autumn, winter. Einstein told us that time is a dimension, it is not a real thing; it is not a material thing you can touch. Evolution does not measure things. You only measure something to give it a meaning for yourself; evolution is an adaption to change. It is not a measure.

Does this mean that when you have created a behaviour you cannot change? Obviously it does not, however, changing some behaviour can prove to be very challenging and often seem impossible. Fears, doubt, guilt, blame, insecurity to name only a few, are all too common challenging behavioural states to change. That is why it is important to understand how your thoughts are formed. To know how to control and move your thoughts, you must know what they are, and how they are being created.

When very young, all thoughts and actions are new. Once new thoughts and actions become memories they can become behaviour. Our existence tends to be strongly influenced by our sub-conscious memory (past behaviour). In an adult human there is a theory that over 99% of actions are driven by internal/external environmental signals triggering memory (past behaviour) learned before. Even new behaviour can be an amalgamation of learned patterns from the past, resulting in a new pattern of behaviour. We are all a product of our past. We have evolved to respond to signals from our internal/external environment; once learned we can sub-consciously respond in the same ways time after time, unless we can recognise that we are following previous learned behaviour. We live from the basis of our sub-conscious memories. Without reflection and contemplation we live our lives based upon our past learned behaviour. So if you keep choosing your future based on what you know then you will only get what you know.

Your thoughts, which become memory, are filed in your sub-conscious, not randomly, not in alphabetical order, not even by time or date; your thoughts are filed in your sub-conscious by emotion. Your sub-conscious creates a file to exactly match the strength of the emotional peptide you create.

Summarizing the last section we could say that a thought is re-cycled information influenced by our many senses. An emotion is a chemical peptide created by you, and is the trigger attached to every thought filed in your sub-conscious memory, enabling response through environmental signals authorising recall of learned behaviour.

I am here, NOW, in a human form,
on Planet Earth.

... *thoughts are a product of environmental signals utilized by the senses, then observed, received, and processed by the brain ...*

Trapped in Amber

Trapped in Amber

Be aware of your emotions while reading the narrative.

DO YOU KNOW HOW AMAZING YOU ARE?

Our anatomy system consists of a skeletal system, digestive system, endocrine system, urinary system, muscular system, lymphatic system, nervous system, autonomic system, cardiovascular system, respiratory system and reproductive system. Each eukaryotic cell has the same anatomy systems as the body. Your cells are alive and each cell functions like a miniature person, including having the ability to think. You have trillions of 'little people' (cells) in your body, and everyone (every cell) responds only to you. For your body to do anything you have to give it an instruction. There is no event or other person that can influence your behaviour unless you authorise it.

The cells in your body are responsible for all the functions of your body. Those cells take instruction only from you. You may not have realised it, but you are perfectly you. You are exactly as you have taught yourself. The choices you have made have created the person you are at this moment, and the circumstances of your life. You attract into your life what you think about the most.

It would never occur to you that over-sleeping, and running late for work could have been part of a bigger plan to delay your departure from the house, which in turn made you a few minutes later in reaching a certain junction on the road. Maybe that short delay saved your life because a driver was going to be distracted at that junction, and would have hit you. Is it impossible to believe that such micro-dramas could continually occur to save your life? We can and often do overrule these small micro-dramas with corresponding consequences. We ignore the fact we have left our umbrella, forgot to check the back door was locked, neglected to say goodbye or I love you. We ignore the stranger in need of help on the other side of the road because we are too busy or late for an appointment.

You might now argue *'What about the person who gets murdered, the soldier who gets killed in war, the child who gets injured in an accident,* surely they were not attracting those events into their lives? There is a controversial response to these questions, and it is; *how can anyone be absolutely sure what someone else is thinking?* Perhaps they were attracting events through their thoughts and behaviour. Not directly but indirectly. If you are reacting to this last statement in an angry or negative way then be aware that the emotion you are feeling has been created by you, because you have placed a value on the words. It is your belief system that is responding; it is something you have taught yourself; it is the reaction of a peptide. Words cannot physically make you do or think anything ... you have to give an instruction to your cells for your body to respond. The words do not magically press buttons or move invisible strings attached to your body to make you respond. Stop blaming other people or events for making you feel or react in anyway; you are responsible for you.

Negative thinking has perverse effects within the Universe. Do you know what a negative thought is? Let me give you an example. If you continually keep telling yourself, 'I want a better relationship, or I want a better job, or I want to feel good about myself; then the Universe will give you exactly what you are asking for. It will keep you wanting a better relationship, wanting a better work role or wanting to feel good about yourself, and keep you wanting, and keep you wanting. If you keep asking to keep wanting, then that is what you will get. Your life is not a mathematical formula that follows rules that say two negatives make a positive.

The Universe does not respond to your words, it responds to your being. If you live your life with fear and doubt inside, but repeat positive affirmations outside, then you will be in conflict with your being. You must speak and feel the life you desire, and live it with a passion. If there is anyone or anything in your life that reduces that passion, then you must remove yourself from those negative vibrations as much as you can to allow your being to live the life you desire. This is your life, not your mother's or your father's, it is not your husband's life or wife's life, or your children's life; you did not come on this planet to work in an office. However, there is a warning that comes with this choice. Remember that whatever your life is now you have attracted that ... this may be a challenging concept for you to understand at this moment, but it is possible that it is so; your belief system is the world in which you will walk.

Ask yourself, 'what is the priority in my life?' You may *want to think* that it is your family; you may even fool yourself into believing that, however, your actions may prove that you consider your career and standing in the work environment more important, as you may consider working hard to be necessary to give your family a *'good life.* Of course you will tell yourself that you are doing what you do for the benefit of the family. Your belief system will blind you in your thinking if you are not aware of how and what you think about. It takes courage and brutal honesty with oneself to determine your reality or the reality of your world. When you have accepted what you are, then you can appreciate that you probably have everything you have asked for ... just not in the way you expected because you took some of the *'other things'* for granted. For instance, you work hard, and the other people in your life therefore, must automatically understand, and they must be subservient to what you believe is the way they should behave. Because you are the bread-winner, this does not give you power to determine the thoughts, ideas, and dreams of others in your family unit. There are consequences to every choice you make, and you will have no control outside yourself.

This is your life, only you can determine how you spend your time on Planet Earth. Every choice and action has consequences. If you desire to be the best mother you can be, then that is wonderful; however you must be prepared for the consequences that your children will grow with desire to live their lives, in their own way, which may not include you in any major part. You might have been the best mother you could have been, but when your children leave home, if you have not retained other desires, you won't be able to live your life based on what you were, a mother living with her children. And you cannot expect your children to live their lives with you at the centre. Your children are not yours to manipulate according to your belief system, they are beings in their own right, and are ultimately responsible for their life on Planet Earth. Ultimately you are responsible for your life only.

You are only a part player in the role of life if you share your life with someone else. Do not expect everything to be as you believe it should be. Accept that your choices will impact on others, as their choices will impact on you; they have to make choices too. It is all about balance. Learn acceptance. ***When you learn acceptance you take responsibility for change, and for your life.***

You have to strive to '*be*' or to have passionate engagement with life. If you're not, you draw into your being, confusion, fear, doubt, anxiety and a feeling of loss, usually with questions such as; what is the purpose of life? Is this all there is? Life is a journey not a destination, it is full of mystery and wonder, or is it a problem to be solved. Or is life a combination of the two; ultimately its only you who decides!

No one can empower or disempower another person in relation to life. When you feel hurt by someone's action or hurt by an event, it is your interpretation, influenced by your belief system that will determined your response. It is not the other person or the circumstance that determines your reaction ... it is you. Many of us are disempowered when we are children, and being children we are unable to realise this. Most children see older people as having wisdom or knowledge that they have not got. This wisdom or knowledge to a child has meaning.

So if you say to a child that they are useless, no good, a liar, not clever or any other negative valued label, then the child will think it is a true reflection, and that signal will be recorded in the child's memory with a corresponding peptide. Repeated labeling of the child will reinforce the peptide chemical in the young person's memory. As they grow the label will become embedded as a behavioural trait, becoming part of what appears to be a facet of the child's personality that the child will accept is something they are, and then of course they try to live up to it. From the child comes the adult. Remember your child could one day be a parent; are you teaching your child how to be a good parent?

The person colouring the child with a negative label has not got special powers that can disempower the child, however, the young person is not mature enough to make healthy, wise, informed or beneficial choices about the signals being received through their senses, and they will literally interpret the signals as being accurate, and as a true reflection of them. Young adults are a reflection of their up-bringing. Remember that children are influenced by many things other than parents; there is television, school, friends, the internet, and many more indirect and direct life events that embed behaviour sub-consciously.

In adults, events and circumstances can change behaviour if that adult does not realise that they can make a choice. Whatever happens you are not forced to think anything, you have to give the instruction to your body through your thoughts for your body to respond. You do not work by magic. Your body's response can be an action, like running away; or an emotion, value, meaning or feeling like fear, doubt, I am not good enough. Often your response to events is both an action and an emotion; these two reactions to your *'instructive thought'* is immediately translated into a peptide by your hypothalamus, and infused into your cellular memory. Initially this is memory, repeated responses to memory becomes behaviour.

Do not seek to satisfy an outward perception, for awakening is within. Grace comes in the space of surrender. The path can only be seen when you ask the right question. If you ask 'how do I get to London?' then you will get directions to London. Ask the question to favor your desire. *When you learn detachment you take responsibility for change, and for your life.*

As you walk through your life you will instruct your belief system to label all events and create emotional responses, teaching your belief system how you want to behave in the future. Your belief system considers that these responses are your desires. Your belief system will remind you of your past desires; your need for fear, doubt, negative self-judgement, or blame, whenever your external signals trigger a similar event. This is a gift that the mind has evolved to give you a memory, allowing you to recall a response to events that you have encountered. This is why behaviour is repeated ... it is an illusion ... events did happen in your past, but that is exactly what they were, events that happened. Only you can keep the memory and the emotional labels (your desires) in your present, by keeping your current belief system.

It must be remembered that in terms of your cell's behaviour, whatever you tell your cells is translated by your cells as your desire. Your cells have no judgement; your subconscious has no judgement, therefore whatever you think, your body responds exactly to your instructions. The mind that gave you the problem cannot give you the solution. Learn control of desires. ***When you learn to control your desires (your taught behaviour) you take responsibility for change, and for your life.***

Strive to be conscious in every moment for you are here ... now ... in a human form ... on Planet Earth. It is understood that the Earth's equator is rotating at around one thousand miles per hour, and it is going around the Sun at about sixty seven thousand miles per hour. However, these speeds are nothing compared with the speed of the rotation of our solar system, which is rotating around our galaxy's center at about four hundred and ninety thousand miles per hour. And if that was not enough, our galaxy is cruising through Space at around six hundred and twenty miles per second. Do not accept the world that you think you see on a day to day basis, for that is mainly only the world from your past, created by you, and remembered by your current belief system. It is an illusion. You can change your illusion of life at anytime; all you have to do is to change your mind. Learn to contemplate the moment. ***When you learn to contemplate the moment you take responsibility for change, and for your life.***

True empowerment of your being, originates behind the eyes, not in front of your eyes, because once power becomes visible it evaporates. If you judge another person or thing then your judgement anchors you to that person or thing, making you its servant. Judge other people or events too harshly, and you become their prisoner. What emotional or mental weight do you carry that is unnecessary to your journey? The truth of the situation is, *'your past does not equal your future'*.

How do you know what success or failure really is? Your belief in what success or failure is... is just that ... your belief system. Your belief system is made up ... it is not real. There is no success or failure, there is only choice. You can never have advanced proof of the outcome of your choices, so do not let fear or doubt bias your journey. You have not got free-will; you are guided by your belief system. Do not limit your time or potential on Planet Earth by wanting ... dream your desire and take action, making each moment part of the journey towards your dream.

Recognise that both the materialistic and idealistic views of life have five desires; the physical, the social, the environment and the economic; all necessary for the psychological. Is it possible that spending time on determining your desires, will result in achieving the potential that is within?

... Acceptance ...

... Detachment ...

... Control of Desires ...

... Contemplation of the Moment ...

Trapped in Amber

Be aware of your emotions while reading the narrative.

HOW DO YOU CHANGE AND LEARN TO DREAM?

Changing your life is easy. Yes easy. Most people start in the wrong place, they start by trying to change things in the outside. You should always start by changing what is in the inside. Let me explain what I mean by the outside and the inside.

Things in the outside are events that happen outside your body, like relationships, work roles, social occasions, family, and friends; they are external experiences, many of which you may feel are unavoidable. Many are controlled by your behaviour, and remember your behaviour is your belief system. Your belief system directs you to do specific things like, go to a place of work you don't particularly enjoy, keep you believing that you are not good enough to do this or do that. Your belief system will attract into your life the type of people who will reinforce your belief system, thus keeping you in the same place. DNA is the foundation memory of the new life-form; all other memory is encoded into the cell by the life-form through interpretation of the sense signals, and the peptide connection

Trapped in Amber

Trapped in Amber

Be aware of your emotions while reading the narrative.

EXERCISE 1: WHAT IS THE MOST IMPORTANT THING IN YOUR LIFE?

Stop reading and consider this question carefully. Do not return to the narrative until you have really thought about your answer. Write your answer down either in the book or on a separate piece of paper. Please do that now. This exercise is important so please spend whatever time you need to consider your response.

Trapped in Amber

What is the most important thing in your life?

When answering this question many people respond by saying that happiness is the most important thing in their life; happiness and enjoyment. You may have heard the saying *'You are only here once so enjoy yourself.'* Unfortunately happiness is a dependent thought. When you seek happiness it is always attached to someone or something being in or out of your life. Happiness is dependent upon someone or something else other than you.

For you to be happy he or she has to love you; for you to be happy you need to get that promotion or that job. For you to be happy you have to overcome your illness. You cannot be happy by yourself ... someone or something else has to be in or out of your life for you to be happy. Therefore you are empowering someone or something else to make you happy.

You may say that your children or family are the most important thing in your life. Again you are measuring your happiness on something that is dependent upon something other than you. You are attaching outcomes to what you do, and those outcomes are not dependent upon you.

It is possible that the most important thing in your life is ... *your health*. Even with health challenges from birth or accidents, you should always strive to be the healthiest body you can be. Being as healthy as you can be is the primary process that determines your opportunities; without your best possible health you are limiting yourself unnecessarily, and you may cause stress and worry in others. What sort of mother/father would you be if you are always ill, stressed, depressed, and angry? If you die prematurely because of your decisions to be unhealthy, how does that tell others that you love them; more to the point, how does that tell you that you love you?

... you may not have realised it, but you are exactly as you have taught yourself ...

Trapped in Amber

Be aware of your emotions while reading the narrative.

EXERCISE 2: WHAT IS THE SECOND MOST IMPORTANT THING IN YOUR LIFE?

Stop reading and consider this question carefully. Do not return to the narrative until you have really thought about your answer. Write your answer down either in the book or on a separate piece of paper. Please do that now. This exercise is important so please spend whatever time you need to consider your response.

Trapped in Amber

Trapped in Amber

What is the second most important thing in your life?

It is possible that the second most important thing in your life is your *peace and well-being* ... your harmony with all other life-forms. Do not seek something that is dependent upon something other than you, and do not attach false outcomes to what you do; do things because you choose to, not because you want the outcome. The only outcomes to living should be Peace and Love.

Peace and Love do not stifle ambition, hard-work, innovation and creativity; they in fact enhance them for the benefit of all life-forms, not just the few. Developing new and better ways to live is not detrimental to Planet Earth or Life; what is detrimental is the process that new developments are concerned only with the accumulation of material wealth for a few. Very few things are produced for the true benefit of Life; most things are produced for profit only. If it does not make a profit then it does not get produced, even if it is sustaining to Life.

The Human animal has developed a belief system that limits survival to competition and not co-operation. It is the value and labels we place on things, which allow selected small groups to control, and have power over the majority of life-forms on the Planet. It is the perceived outcomes of control and power, which have false values of material wealth for the few; driving belief systems of greed, fear, doubt, hate, and many more destructive patterns of behaviour. This is how illness and disease have exploded to touch all our lives. Could it have been different? Could it be different? These are questions for you to reflect upon.

... I am here, NOW, in a human form, on Planet Earth ...

Trapped in Amber

Be aware of your emotions while reading the narrative.

WHY YOU CANNOT HAVE EVERYTHING.

You cannot have everything ... but you can have anything. It is that choice; the choice of choosing what it is you desire from your time, on this wonderful Planet, that will determine your outcome. Change has always come about when enough people made different choices, then over time communities changed, nations changed, and the world changed. Every change starts with you. We all have to make different choices, changing our own world that we have created in our belief system, and then the rest of the population can change.

Your perception of the world, and how it works, is held in your belief system, it is local to you; if you change your belief system you actually change the world. You change the world that you perceive, and that is very relevant, and feels real at the local level of the individual. The people you interact with are then subject to your new behaviour, making them reflect on their own behaviour. We all reflect the world in which we '*walk*'.

Let me ask another question ... remember this is a question for discussion, it is not an opinion, so do not judge or put a value on the question. Retain an open mind. *"Why do things have to be made for financial-profit?"*

For clarification I would like to attempt to define profit. Financial-*Profit is a strategic outcome which is set as the primary pre-condition of producing a product.* The assumption implied from the definition is: Nothing is ever produced and sustained, that does not make a financial-profit, and therefore, nothing is ever produced for the primary benefit of health and well-being. Is anything ever made for the single purpose of sustaining life? A question for you to reflect upon.

We seem to have *'bought into'* the belief system that you cannot improve conditions of life without someone making financial gain. Why does profit have to be money? Why can profit not be defined in terms of allocation of life resources; like food, shelter, and healthcare? Are we suggesting in our hypothesis that if financial-profit was illegal then no one would create new ideas and new products? Perhaps every product should be assessed in terms of how essential it is to a life of Love and Peace; if it is not, then perhaps it should not be produced? We call the current system Democracy, which governs much of the Planet in relation to a majority voting ritual allowing multiple choices to dilute and cloud

Trapped in Amber

issues. In every case the results are always about power and control. After every election there are millions of people who are unsatisfied. Democracy does not work for all the people, it works for groups of people only. Dictatorships do not work for all the people either; the rich get richer and the poor ...

So perhaps we need to re-evaluate how we run our side (the human responsibility) of this enterprise we call Life on Planet Earth. Could it possibly be that no one individual or organisation owns the profit, but that everything is shared equally among the population. This might necessitate that the population has to be limited in size; would that be a bad thing? You reflect and come to your own conclusions.

If we produce something which is believed at the time to have benefits, but after time has elapsed proves not to be; then we should have the ability to stop production worldwide. We pretend to do this through the disguise of government, whereas the truth is that governments need financial-profit to survive. Governments are a product of fear, greed, doubt and insecurity; these are illusions and are not real. Governments pass laws to allow things to be produced that are clearly detrimental to all life on this Planet. Governance of population is a good thing if the primary role is to listen and provide Peace and Love for all life-forms on Planet Earth.

Trapped in Amber

Every person on this Planet is capable of living in Peace and Love with all life; it is only the belief system of the individual that creates differences and conflict. I intend to provide clear evidence that the belief system of every individual on this Planet is made up, and is not real. So by definition, if I have opinions, then they too will be made up by my belief system. I will therefore provide evidence, that will provide you, the reader, with tools and techniques that will allow you to test out and demonstrate your illusionary world view.

When you know that your belief system is made up and illusionary ... then and only then, can you stop believing what you think is real ... you will know it is not. **Do not believe anything ... know it.** Know(ledge) is more powerful than belief or faith.

You can only know something if you **do not** believe it or have a faith in it. Faith and belief are not a measure of understanding; they are a sign of doubt and uncertainty. Stop talking to the cat, and live your life on purpose. Do you want to live your life believing and having faith ... or knowing? And when I say knowing I do not mean blindly knowing, which is a hidden faith, but really knowing, because you have tested it out, and it works every time all the time for every person who participates in the self-discovery. If you do not know, then learn how to free yourself from your current belief system. Read on.

Summary:

Take responsibility for your Planet. You are not separate from the Planet; you are made from the same atoms, you are part of the eco-system of the Planet. You and every life-form on the Planet are connected, and how we all operate together will determine the Planet's health and well-being. Every atom on Planet Earth is star dust. We are Planet Earth.

Trapped in Amber

Be aware of your emotions while reading the narrative.

HOW IS YOUR BEHAVIOUR CREATED?

Your belief system is a product of your many senses; supported by your emotional values, which create chemical peptides, creating memory, and evolving behaviour. This is easy to test out so that you will know this is how you work ... you will not believe it ... you will know it. You should not need faith when it comes to taking responsibility for your actions; you should know that you do not work by magic. There is no one with an electronic controller with your name on, pressing buttons making you say and do anything. You are totally responsible for you. You are perfectly you, as you are exactly what you have taught yourself to be.

Your belief system is created not by the experiences you have, but by what your body senses. Let me prove this to be the case.

How many of you would tie strong elastic bands to your ankles and jump off a high bridge? This is called bungee jumping. Some of you would ... many of you would not.

Those of you who would not, have probably never done it. So if you have never had the experience then why would you not have the experience? Your belief system stops you, Your belief system conjures up reasons why you should not have the experience. Clearly your belief system has been influenced by something other than your bungee jumping experience. Your belief system was not created by your experience. For those of you who have never bungee jumped, but would, then your belief system conjures up reasons why you would have the experience. The same principle applies, and you should ask yourself why, and how does your belief system formulate permission for you to have the experience before actually having the experience?

Your belief system is created by your many senses. It is your belief system that allows you, or does not allow you, to have experiences. The choice, your belief system allows you to make, reinforces your belief system. Your belief system drives the choices you make in your life.

When you have or do not have experiences, this reinforces your belief system. If you keep doing the same thing, or not doing anything, you reinforced your belief system that gives you your personality and behaviour. This then determines the colour and shape of the world you will attract into your life. The loop formed by your belief system, your experiences and your personality and behaviour is often known as *'will power.*

Diagram 1: How Behaviour is created.

How Behaviour is created

Your Environment	CAUSE / EFFECT

Your many Senses

Thoughts Create Your Belief System

INPUT → THROUGHPUT

Experiences
Education
Religion
Eat / Drink
Friends
Read, watch, talk, do
Where you live

Experiences Reinforce Belief System

OUTPUT

WILL POWER

FEEDBACK

Real change can only occur through changes to your external environment

Determines your World & what you will attract into your life

Personality and Behaviour

Mood	Attitude
Choices made	Actions taken
Outcome	Health
Work Skills	Relationships
Standards	Ethics
Value Creation	Achievement

The diagram above may help you to see the relationships between the influences.

Trying to change behaviour by trying to change your experiences have often been described in many ways; hard, laborious, demanding, arduous, strenuous, tough, grueling, tiring, wearisome, exhausting, backbreaking, uphill struggle, formidable, exacting, burdensome, onerous, complex, painful, these are just a few descriptions. One of my clients described it as trying to stir a barrel of honey with a feather. I have to tell you that it is easy to change your behaviour ... yes easy. All you have to do is to change some of the signals being received by your senses, in particular what you hear, see, smell, taste, and touch, (externally triggered senses) and your belief system will automatically change, thus giving you new experiences; this will result in changes in your personality and behaviour.

How many of you have been on a good holiday? Remember what it was like when you were experiencing your holiday? How you felt? How different your outlook on life was, perhaps you had the time to reflect on how you were going to change things when you got back home? Why were your thoughts different? Why did you feel less stressed, less anxious? Was it because you were on holiday? No ... that is not the reason. The reason is because you were sensing different things, and they influenced your existing belief system. Within a short time of returning home, and slipping back into your old routine, those memories (beliefs) would be overruled with your hard-wired previous behaviour. Why? Holidays are a brief change to our normal environment. Could it be to make effective changes it is necessary to remove the old beliefs, and replace them with new ones? When decorating, it is always good practice to remove the old wallpaper before applying a new look, is it not? Or perhaps we should conclude that we should be on holiday all the time? How can you make every moment a holiday? Read on.

How hard can it be to take a car with an engine already in it, and put a new engine in the same place as the old one? Would it not be wise to take the old engine out first, and then replace it? Or perhaps replace some of the old engine parts with new parts? Whichever way, you would need to take parts out before replacing them, yes?

From changing addictive habits like smoking, drinking, drugs and gambling to emotional issues, negative thinking and issues with weight and food; all behaviour is influenced by our senses, combined with our conscious thoughts. Your behaviour is the output from your internal/external environmental signals. To change the output you need to change the input signals. Change your input signals and you change your belief system. Change your belief system and you change your life.

I have many stories of clients who have changed their life by changing the signals from their externally triggered senses. One client, who I will call K, was fifty two years old when he came to see me. He was very depressed and suicidal. After several weeks of working with K, he was able to turn his life around and make significant changes to his working life by going self-employed. He loved it, however, he was two stones over weight, and he was having difficulties with his new work role, as it included getting into small spaces and working with his hands.

I will not detail his story, but needless to say part of the choices K had made in his life had included smoking and drinking alcohol since the age of sixteen. With the help of his wife, they made a list of what he was hearing, seeing, smelling, tasting, and touching, plus some of the other signals from his many senses. For as long as he could remember he had bought a newspaper everyday and read it from cover to cover. Every morning while getting ready for work he had the TV breakfast news programme on. Every night when he returned from work he would listen to the six o'clock news, and again before he went to bed he would listen to the ten o'clock news.

K stopped buying newspapers, and stopped listening to the news on TV, and after seven days he stopped smoking and drinking. He suffered no withdrawal symptoms, and was still able to go out on a regular Friday night with his wife and friends. His friends all smoked and drank alcohol. I saw K two years after this event, and he was still going out with his friends, and had remained a non-smoker, and had never drank alcohol since. Also as a byproduct to K changing his environmental signals he lost over twenty eight pounds in weight within months.

How can a process that involves stopping reading newspapers, and stopping listening to TV news programmes, have an effect of stopping you smoking and drinking? They probably can't, but with other changes of the sense-activated signals K made in his life, he did.

You will need to discover what signals you need to eliminate to make changes in your life. It may appear to be ludicrous to your current belief system, so do not believe it ... try it; test it out for yourself. If you do this as part of the *'How to Change Your Life'* six step programme, detailed later in the book, there is a very strong possibility that you will make different choices, with high probability that those different choices will enhance your life.

Trapped in Amber

Be aware of your emotions while reading the narrative.

HOW IS THE BELIEF SYSTEM FORMED?

You are not born with a belief system, you create it. A new born child up to the age of eighteen months to two years old would generally be in a *trance-like state*. The child up to this age generally is downloading and observing the world. They are not able to form judgements; they exist mostly on internal feelings. The experiences children are exposed to will form the foundation for behaviour. From around two years of age up to seven years of age the child continues to observe and download experiences they have been exposed to, but the brain will start to attach judgmental feelings to events, by creating peptides, to hook memory of events with feelings. When these peptides are triggered by environmental signals, the child will respond without understanding or knowing why.

A child from two years old to seven years of age has the ability to find everything in the world new. They can be fascinated for hours playing pretend games, and observing spiders and worms.

They move from being in a trance to being in a *dream-like state*. These changes can vary depending upon the gender of the child. Generally it is accepted that girls will mature through these stages faster than boys. From around seven years to fourteen years old the child moves into a third stage of development often called the *waking state*. Here they develop consciousness of connection. They begin to understand relationships between things more clearly by testing out learned rules and behaviour. In the dream-like state the child will say 'no'. The child will not necessarily understand the word *'no'*. It is a sound, a word without real meaning as far as the young child is concerned. In the waking state the child will say *'no ... (make me')*. What the child is doing, is asking you to show them how you make someone do something they do not want to do. They are testing out observed and downloaded information.

If the response to the child is shouting, violence or punishment then the child learns that to make people do something they don't want to do you have to shout, use violence or punish. In the waking stage of development the child is asking for information through behaviour. Children often do not know how to ask questions, they do things, and adults often interpret this as rebellion or bad behaviour. To the child, their behaviour is their way of testing things out in an independent way. Children naturally want to become independent ... all infant life-forms develop the need to become independent; it is a necessary part of the life-cycle. Doing things is part of learning; we must remember that the child is operating from their belief system for that is the only way a life-form can operate. No child is born with the rules as interpreted by the parent. Bred into every life-form is the instinct to learn independently about their environment; it is the survival instinct. Behaviour is a child's communication language.

You can read all the books in the world about the game of golf, but unless you try to play the game you will never be a good golfer. Knowledge is not just about reading or being told, it is about doing and experiencing. It is about working out alternatives, choices and consequences, this is only achieved through the signals of your many senses; for only these influences will affect the belief system of the life-form, and all life-forms behave only according to their belief system. If you tell children what to do all the time they will never be able to test out their learned behaviour, and they will never be able to be independent of control and the past.

The next stage of development of the belief system is the *consequential-thinking state,* and this is reached between the age of twelve to fourteen years of age. Here the child starts to form consequential thinking skills about alternative strategies and consequences of actions. What could happen if ? If I do this it could result in that? How can I do this or how can I get that? Understand that this is the start of the process of understanding; it is not a step change in the child. There is no upper limit of age to the consequential-thinking state; some people may never attain appropriate consequential thinking skills. There are many reasons for this, often stemming from childhood where signals received from the child's environment wired a belief system of abuse and neglect. This can lead to pedophiliac tendencies in adult hood or the inability to love and care.

There are two more states of *'being'* following this that have no age range either, but rarely occur before the age of fourteen, often not developing at all. The 5th stage in the formation of the belief system is called a *state-of-peace*. This is where the individual acknowledges that their health and well-being are the most important elements of their life. They change their life-style to accommodate healthy dietary habits, and meditative practices. It is a stage when a person asks the question when conflict enters their life ... *"Do I want to be right or do I want Peace?* The choice they make determines their outcome. Choose *"I want to be right,"* and inevitably there is conflict. Choose *"I want Peace,"* and their life will change. Choosing Peace does not mean letting people walk all over you, or being weak. It takes great strength to allow someone else to be in their illusionary world created by their belief system, and for you to control your desires (of wanting to be right).

Change in belief system comes only by question; and often the question is to self, stimulated by one or more of the many externally triggered senses. The final stage in the development of the belief system is the *'state of knowing'*. This is a state of wisdom about the illusionary elements of being in a living form on Planet Earth. The *state of peace* and the *state of knowing* are not places ... they are a practice.

Your belief system is a product of your environmental signals ... your many senses. Your environmental signals drive your new conscious thoughts, hooked together with their emotional values and meanings; or your learned sub-conscious thoughts already pre-loaded with emotional values and meaning, dictate your behaviour.

No person is evil or bad, they are just living life through their belief system. We are not born with a belief system; it is something which is created by a process of exposure to externally triggered senses, which allow thought to anchor an emotion, value or meaning to an event, allowing our brains to record the memory and desired action. Behaviour in a growing child is an instinctive learning drive. In the adult, behaviour is mostly driven by previous instructions to the sub-conscious, determined by past environmental signals received through the senses. Generally adults live in the control of their learned behaviour; they live in the past. The world they see and *'believe in'* is a vision of past interpretations, manipulated to fit the current event, which attracts around them a world matching the vision held within their belief system.

Diagram 2: How the Belief System is Formed.

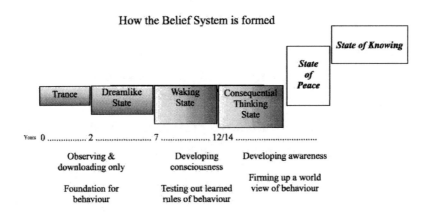

We grow in our life-garden like flowers in a soil that is nurtured by fear, doubt, hate, insecurity and pain, watered by illusion. We tend our gardens with high fences and locked gates, fearful of change, which is often seen as bad (weeds).

If you live your life telling yourself that you *'ought to'* do this or you *'ought to'* do that, then you are living your life on the edge of a volcano. Your suicidal life-style will result in breakdown and collapse.

Perhaps you are a '*have to*' person? Your mind is always telling you that you '*have to*' do this or '*have to*' do that. You are in survival mode running on stress, waiting for your turn to have the breakdown. You are probably always tired and run-down, lost within your belief system in a world of pressure, believing you have insufficient resources.

Are you the '*need to*' person? Striving for security, always anxious about the future; worrying things into existence; living in future problems.

The '*want to*' person is the social animal who lives to impress others, hiding behind insecurity, fear and doubt. Feeds on pressure to conform to what they think others expect of them.

These first four questioning-types trap themselves in their developing belief system. They develop awareness of the world that they continually attract into their life. The world works exactly as they perceive it to work, and they continually attract people around them who confirm this view. Stepping into the 5th stage of belief development needs a different approach.

You need to start '*desiring to*' do things and *desiring to* change things about yourself. To desire is a form of love, and this will enhance your self-esteem and enjoyment of things that you do.

Then perhaps you can take a big step and *'choose to'* do the things in your life. This is all about empowering yourself, self-fulfillment and respect for you.

This is the step before you finally walk into your life with the words *'love to'* appearing before everything you do. When you *love to* do the things you do and you *love to* live your life the way you are living it, then you have attained self-actualization, and you are on the way to peace, passion, and knowing.

... change your belief system and you change your life ...

Trapped in Amber

Be aware of your emotions while reading the narrative.

IS LIFE A MIRACLE?

Do you find yourself responding to this heading in a negative way? Are you saying in your head ... yes it is? Let me ask you a question. When you think in your mind, whose voice do you hear? Has it got an accent? Now are you ready for the next question? The voice in your head is only in your head ... correct? How can you hear silence?

EXERCISE 3: LIFE IS A MIRACLE
Please complete the following short exercise.

STATEMENT	YES	NO
The birth of a child is a miracle		
The birth of a rat is a miracle		
The birth of a cockroach is a miracle		
The birth of a mosquito is a miracle		
The birth of a fly is a miracle		
The birth of a virus is a miracle		

If some of your answers to *Exercise Three* were *'Yes'*, and some *'No'*, then this is proof that you are living in your belief system. If all your answers were *'Yes'*, then again proof that you are living in your belief system. The unemotional answer to all the questions is *'No'*. All life is a matter of the right conditions.

A miracle is defined as a phenomenon, something that happens that should not have happened under normal circumstances. Life is not a miracle. We may not as yet completely understand how everything works, and there will probably always be some element of the chemical process which is beyond our comprehension, in that chemical reactions happen. We actually do not always understand why, but we accept that they do because it happens repeatedly. Life happens repeatedly if the conditions are right. Different life-forms will happen when the circumstances change.

Life is not a miracle; it is a process that happens all the time every time when the conditions are right. It is an observable and rigorously evidenced probability. It has nothing to do with a divinity or an outside controlling force. It is a fundamental rule of the Universe ... when conditions are right, life will appear.

Life is a result of biological evolution, chemicals mixing together over and over again through a time period of billions of years. It is only because we have placed a value on birth, a meaning, an emotion, that has created a peptide that has informed our belief system that we think life is a miracle. It is not real, it is only what we want to accept and believe. In terms of the Universe, *'life'* is a reaction to environmental conditions. When those environmental conditions change, then life-forms will change or disappear. This is not a miracle. What is amazing is that some life-forms have the ability to imagine and dream. However, the ability to dream has consequences.

How are you feeling at this moment? Notice the emotions and thoughts that your belief system is re-creating in your mind, and the peptides that are flooding your body. Interesting isn't it that some readers will think what they are thinking is real, and will not associate any of their thoughts or feelings to peptides, and belief system even though they have read this far. They will selectively forget or ignore what is happening inside their bodies, choosing to believe that what they think and feel is true. If that is so, you are thinking with your logical consequential thinking belief system. You are living in a world with opinions that are fixed within boundaries of comfort. You are living exactly as you have taught yourself. You are perfectly you.

Regardless of how you are thinking and feeling please read on, because it is possible for you to understand that you are being controlled by your past. **Know**ledge should be accepted without the colour of your prejudices and beliefs. When you understand the new knowledge, you should balance it with your many senses, and decide if the new knowledge relates to what you can actually experience, hopefully that will be a state of peace.

Life being a miracle or not is only a point of view, depending upon your knowledge, and how you have interpreted that knowledge. It is not just about knowledge; it is about how your belief system uses that knowledge. When we accumulate knowledge, what we have taught ourselves to do is to assess it, categorize it, then ascribe value to it according to the meaning it has for us, and then measuring that to see if it fits in with our current belief system values. Only then will we establish if we are going to apply the knowledge, to change behaviour.

New knowledge is a frightening concept as it means, "I could be wrong." The older you get the more frightening the concept of change becomes with the implied notion of 'a wasted life'. This may lead many to hold onto a belief or faith as a security blanket, telling themselves perhaps that they don't understand the latest science, which is after all only the best guess or understanding that rigorous experimentation can show. However, they do understand a concept of believing in an invisible entity, or living behind a barrier of *'ignorance is bliss'*. Can you understand that some people just don't care? Like water, they find the route of least resistance, because change has to destroy before it can flower. We should remember that it is not where you start on your journey, but where you finish.

Consider the following two statements.

There is a God.

There is no God.

Do any of the statements make you feel an emotion? Are you happy at reading statement one, and upset or annoyed at statement two? Does statement two make you feel alone? Is it because of that feeling of loneliness that you prefer statement one?

Question! How can words written on a page (above) have the power to make you feel anything? Do the words have control over your body? Is the statement so wrong in your belief system that your body automatically responds to the words? If they do then you are an addict ... addicted to your belief system, which is made up, and is not real.

Has the last statement generated an emotional feeling in your body? Do you think you work by magic? Do you think that emotion is something created by your God? Because you think or feel something, does that mean it is real? Is it possible that if religion (any religion) was invented today, it would be rejected out-of-hand as make-believe or magic? Religion is our connection to an ancient world of ignorance and superstition. If you let your belief system live in the past then can you guess what your future will be?

I can understand that many readers will find it challenging to accept that there is no rigorous scientific proof that a God exists or has ever existed. There is no proof that a God has not existed either. There is no rigorous scientific proof either way. For people to make it so, all they have to do is believe it. If they believe it, does it make it real? The last two statements are questions; they are for you to answer.

There is very strong evidence that life has evolved and is still evolving, and that the Planet Earth is some five billion years old; that evidence is only the best guess or understanding that science and philosophy have at this moment. It is never classified as 'truth' which will not or can not change. Scientific knowledge is at best testable theory.
It is no wonder as people get older they find it increasingly challenging to change. Consider the process.

The journey of life begins when the sperm of the male and the egg of the female meet in the right conditions. Within a few hours the sperm and egg fuse together setting in motion an elaborate sequence of chemical reactions. Slowly, over a short time limbs, and organs grow, then the brain develops, connecting its special neuron cells into complex patterns. The shape of the body starts to take form. Theory at this moment suggests that the cells of the fetus, adopt the shape of the parent, due to the morphogenetic field of the parent. So humans do not give birth to rabbits even though the process and chemicals involved are the same.

After nine months, changes occur in the parent, and the new life-form is born. The environment of the womb, the hormones circulating around the fetus, affects the development of the new life-form by switching specific genes on or off while still inside the womb. When the baby is born the new environment outside the womb again will cause specific genes to be switched on and/or off. In the outer womb environment, the brain starts to make millions of connections each day as the baby's senses communicate with the brain.

The baby has had no input with regards to the make-up of its genes. You choose none of the initial material that makes your body. All of the cellular material is programmed to adjust to your internal/external environment. The baby is now actually being programmed in-line with its environment, and because it has limited control over any of its functions, the baby is subject to the environmental bombardment of belief forming signals into which it is born.

The baby is now subject to the development stages in *Diagram 2: How the Belief System is Formed (page 108)*. It's possible to see that as a process of growing in the mother's womb, and being born, the baby emerges via an immersion of chemical controlling stimuli, none of which are in the control of the infant, all of which will determine its foundational belief system. For some this experience is an acceptable way to develop, for many others who are subject to poverty, stress, abuse, and neglect, it informs the basis of a different belief system, a different way to view the world, and a different way to behave.

Here you are then, a human life-form made up of cells that you had no part in, programmed by an environment that you had no say in, addicted to foods you had to eat to stay alive, and lacked nutritional knowledge about any health issues and long-term effects. At some point you are expected to take responsibility for yourself. Then you wonder why you often find yourself responding automatically to situations and events without any apparent control over your behaviour. This is put down to your personality. Life is no longer the miracle you imagined it to be. It is exactly what it is. Cellular life-forms like you and me have evolved over many millions of years, with the ability to memorize and recall stimuli, those signals which we've downloaded to create behaviour, necessary for our survival.

You are made from atoms formed in the stars, you are a Child of the Universe, and as such you are wonderful; you are potential; for every cell in your body only obeys you. Yes ... you actually control your body. Your body does exactly what you tell it to do. And you tell your body what to do by the things your body senses, which influence your conscious-mind, which stimulates a thought to which you then attach a value, based on your current belief system. This produces the peptide that will encode the 'desired' belief, and action into your sub-conscious (memory), thus building your behaviour. For the first fourteen to sixteen years of life the external signals are significantly controlled by your family, school and social circumstances. It is the human life-form model that we *'nurture and control'* our children's formative years. The child has little input into what he or she hears, sees, smells, tastes, or touches and indeed, including most of the other senses. The child has little input, when it comes to developing their own belief system.

It is only when, and indeed if the child leaves home, perhaps going to University or College, or perhaps getting a work role that takes them into a new environment, that their independent learning begins. However, their independent learning is coloured with the imposed foundational belief system of childhood. The adult will bloom or wither depending upon its ability to work out an appropriate response to the new sensory signals of the adult world.

You have not got different behavioural systems in your body; you work one way, all the time, every time. Everyone can change. Everyone starts from the same place; you start with what you have, and who you are now, and you possess the ability to change, right now, even in the next moment. The challenge you will have will be that you will not know what to change in the next moment. Everyone knows what it is they don't desire in their life, but few actually know what they do desire, until they really start to reflect. Notice the word is *'desire'* not the word *'want'*.

Remember if you don't want something, then that is your desire, and the Universe will keep you in the place where you don't want it. This is perverse I know, but this is how it works. You must know what it is you desire, for if you don't then how will the dream materialize?

I have developed an exercise to begin the verbalization of your desires. I call it Focused Insight Reflecting on ME (FIRM for short). You ask yourself basic questions., however, you must be firm and honest with yourself and not wishy washy.

Trapped in Amber

... you are perfectly you ...

Trapped in Amber

Be aware of your emotions while reading the narrative.

EXERCISE 4: FOCUSED INSIGHT REFLECTING ON ME (FIRM)

Question 1.
Summarize in no more than one hundred and fifty words your story of how you got to this point in your life.

Sit down in a quiet place and reflect on your journey to date. Do not start writing an essay. Summarize your life experiences by writing headings or short descriptions. Make it a time-line; put things in order and if you can, mention your age at the time of the event. Then look at what you have said, and summarize it into no more than one hundred and fifty words. Use short headline sentences and phrases. It is not an essay. As an example you could start by writing;

My childhood was ..... (filled with memories of ....)

My school days were ....

When I was   ..... (this happened to me)

When I was at ...... (this happen to me)

My mother was ......

My father was ....

Don't forget to put the good down as well as the bad. You should aim to complete it in one go. You should not dwell on the issues of your life, just write them down in heading form. This could take no more than fifteen minutes.

Question 2.
Now put your story into one sentence.
This should take no more than ten minutes.

Question 3.
Now describe yourself as you were (are) in question 1, using separate descriptive words. Use between three and six words only.
This should take no more than ten minutes.

The next part of the exercise requires that you spend time understanding what it is you desire of your life.

Question 4.
Reflect upon your story in question 1, and again in no more than one hundred and fifty words, summarize how you would change your story so that you could be what you desire to be right now.

This is usually where the challenges begin, because most people do not actually know what it is they desire in their life. Now be careful here because this is about you, not about conditional things that you think would make your life better like money or someone to love you. This is asking the question *"what do you desire to be"* not what you desire in your life. This will take whatever time it takes.

Question 5.

From this moment forward how would you like to change your immediate future? What would you like to be different about you, so that you could become who you desire to be?

Again this is about you, not about finding a new job, or finding a new partner, or having more money, although ultimately it may result in all these things. It is about you as a person. Read the question several times so that you understand what it is asking. From this moment on, how could you change something about you, so that you can become who you desire to be? This will take whatever time it takes.

Question 6

Using your answers from question 5, in no more than one hundred and fifty words tell the story of the new you.
This should take no more than fifteen minutes.

Question 7

Now describe the new you, using separate descriptive words.
Use between three and six words only.

This should take no more than ten minutes.

After doing Exercise Four, you will probably be asking yourself *"How do I change?"* The answer to this question is that there are six simple steps to changing your life. Read on.

... it is not where you start on your journey, but where you finish ...

Trapped in Amber

Be aware of your emotions while reading the narrative.

HOW TO CHANGE YOUR LIFE.

I would recommend the following processes and techniques

STEP ONE: KNOW WITH A PASSION WHAT IT IS YOU DESIRE TO BE EVERYDAY OF YOUR LIFE.

This is challenging, as most clients who come to me, know what it is they don't want, but few if any know what it is they actually desire. Understand that this can and often does change, as you progress on your journey of life on Planet Earth. Desires or dreams often only last for a few years, and as we achieve them we then change; for those with passion, this change is a continuous cycle. Remember that life is a journey not a destination. Never stop living; even on the day you die always have another book to read or another smile to give. Set your desires in line with your abilities; don't start believing in magic.

Trapped in Amber

STEP TWO: LEARN HOW TO MEDITATE EVERYDAY OF YOUR LIFE.

There are many forms of meditation, and there are various definitions of what meditation is and is not. I produce meditation CD's for clients, and for my own personal use, using Brainwave Entrainment software in all cases. You can meditate without the use of a CD by learning how to focus the mind and reflect in silence. Meditation is wonderful in that it is free, other than if you want to use a CD to assist you. It is very effective very quickly, especially with reducing stress and anxiety. However, without the use of meditation CD's it can take practice, and some people find it difficult to 'get into' a meditative state.

I use Brainwave Entrainment CD meditation because it allows me to help clients to meditate with ease, and is almost guaranteed to work. As I produce my own CD's they provide a high quality of meditation that is consistently repeatable.

When you practice meditation on a regular basis (I recommend daily), your heart rate and breathing will slow down, your blood pressure normalizes, you will use oxygen more efficiently and you will sweat less. Your adrenal glands will produce less cortisol, and your immune system improves. Your mind will clear and creativity increases. People who regularly meditate often find that they can reduce or eliminate negative habits like smoking, drinking alcohol, and drugs.

In all cases you should use meditation to improve your health and well-being by taking time in the meditation to communicate with your body. Remember your cells only obey you, and in meditation you have the full attention of every cell. With practice you can heal many problems of the body, attaining an abundance of health.

A benefit of using a well produced and effective meditation CD is that it will give you control over the time you meditate. Most people find their main excuse for not meditating is that they have not got time. Using a well produced CD means that it should wake you up at the end of the meditation, after say an allotted period of thirty minutes; therefore you can fit your meditation into your busy day with confidence that you can rejuvenate your mind and body. Meditating for longer durations is definitely recommended when you have no time constraints, but controlled meditation time slots is probably the most effective way to begin changing your health, well-being and life. Setting aside the time to reflect in silence into your daily routine, can only be beneficial for you.

Trapped in Amber

STEP THREE: LEARN HOW TO SET INTENTIONS EVERYDAY OF YOUR LIFE.

I am now going to tell you about something you have been doing most of your life; however, you have probably not realised what you have been doing or how powerful the effect is of what you have been doing. Confused? Let me explain. It's Monday morning, and the alarm goes off, you are dragged from your sleep struggling to orientate your mind to the day of the week. Is it Sunday? No, you have to go to work or do whatever role your Monday mornings bring. Your mind races with the painful thoughts of those tasks, and the fact that this is going to be one of those typical hectic, boring, stressful days, and its raining.

Have you got the picture or should I say, is it possible that this could be the picture you are creating in your mind, of what your day could be or is going to be like? At the end of the day when you are preparing for bed, and you reflect on your day, was it like you had imagined or was it worse? And as you reflect are you setting up the stress, and pain of the days to come?

You are actually attracting into your life the events and situations you are thinking about. They may not be exactly as you thought they were going to be, but the underlying stress, boredom, tiredness and mundane pain of your life-style vibrates all around you. Still you have the holidays to come, if only you had the money.

What most people do every day when they wake up is they prime their body and mind, to how they are going to be during the day. Stressed, bored, feeling something is missing from their life, hating the journey, the work, possibly the people. Day after day they repeat this mantra, and day after day their life is exactly what they get.

Learn to set *intentions* that are empowering and inspiring, and your day will be so. This is not woo woo or magic, this is how we create our lives. We see the world through the coloured glass of our belief system, and we reinforce this illusion through repetition and behaviour. The world is exactly as you think it is, but what you think, is not real. It is an illusion, built from your accumulated environmental signals, which have informed your belief system, which keeps on attracting the world around you that you keep thinking about. Why don't you attract into your life something else? How? By setting intentions and creating your day.

This is not a process that will change your work role from being boring to wonderful, or stop the boss from being a bully, or change your partner into what you desire them to be. Setting intentions will change you. You will change the way you think about the negative elements in your life, and then you will find possibilities to change.

How to set intentions and create your day.
Do you know what your intentions for life are? Well before you can set them you need to know what they are. Can you remember what the most important thing in your life was? *Health.* What was the second most important thing in your life? *Peace.* Well health and peace should be the first two intentions you set everyday.

I set my intentions twice a day; every morning before I get up, and every night before I go to sleep. Let me tell you the process. I have a clock radio and CD player next to my bed, which I programme to wake me up at 6.00 a.m. every day, including weekends. I programme the CD to come on at this time playing soft incidental spiritual music. The soft music slowly and very quietly drifts into my consciousness. I do not open my eyes I stay warm and cosy in my bed. In my mind I create the silent voice that says in my mind ... *'Thank you for this day. I have another fantastic day on Planet Earth awaiting me. Today is going to be wonderful.'*

I am not saying thank you to God or indeed, any Divinity, I am saying thank you to the Universe because I am a Child of the Universe. Now some may say that all I am doing is substituting the Universe for a 'God Entity'. Well in actuality I'm not, because there is a significant difference

Trapped in Amber

between the two. A 'God Entity' is a belief. There is no proof that a God exists, and there is no proof that one does not exist. A 'God Entity' is an excuse for ignorance, control, dogma, fear, doubt, insecurity and regrets. There is proof that the Universe exists, and there is well accepted understanding that the Universe is made of the same atoms as everything on Planet Earth. I am in essence thanking myself.

There is a consensus within the scientific community that the Universe is conscious; it is not understood at this moment how or why this is so ... it is only the best guess or understanding that we have at this moment. Why do I talk to the Universe as if it can hear me? Because I have tested this process out, and I have a knowing ... not a belief ... that the Universe responds. There are too many serendipitous moments in my life to be accounted for by coincidence alone. I am the Universe in a human form living on a Planet we have called Earth. This is a name we have given to the Planet; it is a label that does not exist within the paradigm of the Universe. Just because man has named something does not make it so; it only makes it a vehicle for human communication, not understanding.

The current accepted understand is that everything in the Universe came from a singularity, a single particle. It is our understanding that anything that comes from a single particle is 'entangled' forever. Planet Earth, and all its forms are entangled with the Universe; it is not possible to be anything else. My human form has developed a degree of complexity, part of which is the ability to communicate. It is the best guess or understanding that through meditative practice and specific actions, human consciousness can communicate with the source; the source of course is The Universe. This knowledge has been tested by me, and I have come to know it is so. I do not believe it ... I know it. You have to test this out for yourself. The printed words on the pages of this book are a guide, a sign-post, an invitation for you to grasp a wonderful opportunity, to change or alter the direction of your life.

I then allow the silent voice in my mind to set my intentions for the day.

The words 'soul' and 'spirit' are words very often used with strong religious connections, and therefore I now do not use them in setting my intentions. You can set as many intentions as you wish, and I would encourage you to start every intention with the same words. *'I am so grateful now for the abundance of ....'* The reason for this is simple. At this moment in time you may be ill, in fact you may have a terminal illness, whatever your state of health at this moment, then it is the way it is. You have everything you have at this moment; therefore for you that is abundance. It is no good comparing yourself to others; you are responsible for you and only you. Do not look outward; be grateful for what is within. Do not set intentions for a future that you have no control over ... do not live your life believing in magic. By saying your intention is to be healthy, the Universe will grant your wish, and keep your health so that you are always intending to be healthy, it will not make you healthy.

You may have very little money, but whatever you have that is what you have, therefore to you at this moment that is abundant. Do not wish for what others have, do not live your life believing anything. Know that you are responsible for your life, you and only you. Be grateful for the abundance of everything you have in this moment. Set you intentions everyday in gratitude of that abundance, and it will grow.

Intentions can be specific or grouped. You may wish to say the following intentions.

I am so grateful now for the abundance of all the wonderful things in my life, my health, my peace, my financial wealth, and the love and friendship of my family and friends.

These words convey four intentions, and if actions are in-line with the words they can form the basis for change in your life.

STEP FOUR: LEARN HOW TO CREATE YOUR DAY EVERYDAY OF YOUR LIFE.

Now remember I am still in bed with my eyes closed. I may slip into a short sleep and slowly wake again to my soft music. I then create my day by saying ...

"When I get up and start my day I will feel wonderful, confident, self assured, calm and relaxed. Make it so."

I am not talking to the Universe with these words; I am talking to the cells in my body. The words 'make it so' are the instruction to my body to follow my desire. I may slip back into sleep, but guess how I feel when I get up and start my day?

I do something similar when I go to bed. I prepare for bed and when I decide to settle down, lights go out and I snuggle up, I then say in my silent mind the following;

"Thank you for this day ...." I may reflect upon my day for example ... *today I was laid off, someone stole my car, and the house burnt down. Thank you for those experiences I do not know why I have had them, but thank you.*

Special note ... do not label or put meaning to any experience you have. Do not say it was bad, good, black or white; accept it as an experience only. If you label it then it will become part of your behavioural patterns, and you will start to affect your behaviour. You may get depressed or make yourself ill through worry. Acceptance of what has actually happened without personalizing thc cxperience, empowers you to be in control of you, your life and your situation. Experiences are learning events only; choose to have them consciously and deliberately, not chemically inflicted. Detach from meaning. Things happen, so they happen; do not give them value other than peace and love. Always choose your health and peace in this moment as more important than any past event. Be grateful for what you have in this moment for that is all you have. Do not develop a thought process of *'wishing'* for miracles or magic things to happen.

Next I will say my intentions; they may be the same as what I said in the morning, but you can change them at any time by addition or deletion if you so require.
Then my silent mind will say;
"Clear my mind of all thoughts I am going to drift into a deep, peaceful, restful sleep to wake refreshed and ready for the start of my new day. Do that now."

The words 'do that now' are the instruction to your body. Then with every breath I breathe out I say in my mind the word ***"calm"*** and slowly drift into that deep, peaceful, restful sleep. If any thoughts do appear in my mind I simply say ... *"Clear my mind of all thoughts I am going to sleep ... do that now."*

You must remember the first time you do this your sub-conscious-mind will probably not do exactly as you say, because it has always behaved in a different way, and it will remind you of what you have habitually done in the past. Be patient, your sub-conscious-mind is not your enemy. It is there to protect you, and will respond to the external signals of you going to bed preparing for sleep or getting up in the morning, in the way that you have taught it. You now have to re-educate your sub-conscious-mind to protect you in a more empowering way. It may take days, possibly weeks, but it will change. You do not work by magic, your body is under your control, it always was, and always shall be. Do not believe it ... know it ... go on try it, see how really fantastic you are.

With setting intentions comes another small daily exercise. The first time you see your reflection in a mirror every morning, you must look yourself straight in the eyes, and say aloud; "(Your first name) I love and approve of you."

This is not to practice narcissism or become conceited in your image; this process is a means for you to communicate directly with your human form, demonstrating appreciation and respect for the reflection looking back at you. If you cannot love and respect who you are (not who you want to be) then it is not possible to love and respect anything. You cannot give what you haven't got.

You should try and do this 'mirror work' at least three times a day, if possible. Do it first thing in the morning and last thing at night, with as many times as you can through the day. At first you may find it false; you may feel the words are fake or insincere, but do it, and keep doing it. It may take time, but eventually you will do it and say "Yes I do ... I do love and approve of myself." The change has well and truly begun. I consider mirror work an essential process in the journey of change.

What is the difference between Thoughts, Ideas, and Intentions? Thoughts that are internalised with feelings, emotions or values and outcomes attached, stimulate chemical reactions becoming embedded as memories, enabling recall of behaviour.

Ideas or dreams are thoughts that remain external to the body and do not have feelings, emotions, values or outcomes attached, and they remain flexible with infinite possibilities.

Intentions are internal instructions to the body not triggered by an external environmental signal; they do not have feelings, emotions, values or outcomes attached as they are a grateful acknowledgment of acceptance and responsibility for what is.

STEP FIVE: LEARN HOW TO MOVE AND CONTROL YOUR NEGATIVE AND UNDESIRABLE THOUGHTS EVERYDAY OF YOUR LIFE.

Ever since you gained the ability to think your own thoughts you have been building your belief system, your memory, your behaviour. Your body works one way. It does not have a complicated array of different thought processing systems as your sub-conscious has no judgement, and therefore could not determine any differences in any of your thoughts. It would not be able to distinguish between a negative or positive thought. It would not be able to determine any difference between an angry thought, and a pleasant thought. Your thinking process treats all thoughts exactly the same, all the time, every time; it treats them as your instructions as to how you want your body to behave. It treats your thoughts as your desires.

You are in charge of the body form ... but you are not your body. So who are you? First let us establish that you are in your body. Close your eyes and think of someone you love or someone you like a lot. Think of a place you like, think of something you have done that made you feel good. Think of something wonderful. Get a vision of it in your head ... feel it ... smell it ... make the colours brighter, try and get the feeling of being part of the picture. Take a little time and do that now before you read any further.

OK did you get a good strong picture in your head? What was happening? If you close your eyes, and deliberately think of someone or an event, your brain can form a picture for you to focus on. It will also authorise the hypothalamus to produce the chemicals to match the memory, making you feel the occasion. You see, your brain does not know the difference between what you see, and what you think about.

The organs inside your body have no idea what is going on in the outside world. The only contact the outside world has with your body is through your externally triggered senses; these signals are received by your brain, and your brain produces a picture inside your head. This picture of the world is constantly being shown to you by the brain. Now did you realise that you do not actually see out of your eyes? Your eyes only let light waves in; they do not let anything out. The cones and rods in the retina convert light rays into electrical signals, and send them to the brain through the 1.2 million nerve fibres in the optic nerve.

You do not see with your eyes; what you see is a picture the brain makes from all the signals it receives. The human brain has evolved vision as its primary sense. That is vision defined as the ability to detect light waves. It is not possible for the eyes to project an image outside your body so that you can see the world in three dimensions. The brain creates the image somewhere inside itself; and this image is in three dimensions. Somehow the brain is able to project this image as if it is outside the body. There is currently no scientific understanding of how the brain does this. Perhaps the image is formed in the brain then an *'observer'* looks at the image. The brain is working like a headset of a virtual reality game, which allows you to immerse yourself in the experience. Who or what is the *'observer'*? Blind people develop other senses as their primary way of 'seeing' the world.

If you close your eyes and think ... use your imagination ... visualise ... you can trigger the brain to reproduce an image; often triggering externally influenced senses like smell, taste, touch, sound, and motion. These can enhance imagination and visualization. This implies that your brain will not only respond to your external signals, but it will respond to your thoughts, creating a peptide, creating memory. By closing your eyes you are shutting off the light signals entering the brain; your brain will then take your 'thought instruction' and compensate, generating the image you 'think' you are seeing. Many times the brain can make this thought image very realistic with incredible detail, other times it may be hazy or non-existent, it depends on how good your instructions are, and your ability to practice recalling memory from the sub-conscious. The more you practice this skill the better you get.

With your eyes open the brain produces a three dimensional picture of the world inside your head, and then somehow through an illusion or function of the brain, projects that image in front of you. It is like you are in a black space, and your brain projects an image in three dimensions on a screen that surrounds you. Nothing is coming out of your eyes; your brain creates an image inside the brain, to which you respond. If it were not for light, bouncing off all the different objects, at various wavelengths giving you colour, shapes, density, a sense of dimension, then you would have no need for eyes, and we would have evolved another primary sense to survive.

From the exercise you did a few moments ago when you closed your eyes and thought of someone you love, or a special event, and you got a picture of the person or event in your mind; who exactly, was looking at the picture in your head? Who is the observer? (See page 54)

OK you need time to think about this ... perhaps you are not your body, but your body is the vehicle for you to experience life on Planet Earth? Try this small experiment to prove to yourself that you do not see everything because you have a blind spot in each eye. The brain and the eyes have a special interrelationship that is often not appreciated. Whilst most people may think that what we 'see' comes through our eyes, the current understanding is that much of what we see is information from all our senses being translated by our brain; things that our eyes never actually see. The brain takes that information and creates a picture. So it is actually the brain that sees.

The following simple exercise will provide proof of the blind spots in your eyes.

Above you will see a white circle on a grey background and a white star on a grey background. Hold the page at arm's length with your right hand, and cover your left eye (or close your left eye. Look at the white circle using your right eye. You can clearly see both shapes even though you are focusing your right eye on the white circle. Keep looking at the circle with your right eye. Now slowly bring the page closer to your eyes. At some point, the star will vanish, then if you keep moving the book closer it will reappear again. Move the book very slowly. You can switch and cover your right eye, then with your left eye looking at the star if you move the book closer, the circle will disappear.

"So what?", you may say. Well there are two very interesting things happening. One, why does one shape disappear then reappear? It is because both of our eyes have a blind spot. Two, the brain automatically compensates for that blind spot by filling in a common background; that is why when the shape disappears, you can see the colour of the background instead of the shape. Think about this ... if your eyes did not see the shape how could it see the background? Your brain made it up! You can change the background colours with the same results.

The point of the exercise you have just done was to demonstrate that you can actually know things about yourself and the world, instead of having to believe in your belief system's beliefs about yourself and the world. It's about arriving at a new level of understanding, whereby you KNOW how intimately your body and mind work together, making you an awesome life-form with incredible abilities. Most of the time you take these amazing abilities for granted, letting the autonomic systems of the body react to internal/external environmental events, through past learned behaviour. I now wish to show you how you can actually control many of the autonomic systems of your body, including how to control your thoughts. In fact I am going to show you how to delete the thoughts that are detrimental to your health; those thoughts that keep you trapped in past negative behaviour.

First of all let us prove to ourselves that we can control some of the autonomic processes of the body. Breathing is an autonomic process; it is controlled by the hypothalamus. Try this exercise. Slowly breathe out then slowly breathe in, then breathe out again then breathe in again. Now hold your breath ... hold your breath for at least ten seconds then breathe out and breathe normally.

Do you normally breathe like that? Of course you don't, what you have actually done is interfere with your breathing. You deliberately interfered with your breathing and took control away from your hypothalamus. You could not have continued controlling your breathing in this way because you would need to concentrate on surviving, and what about when you wanted to sleep?

What this simple exercise has shown is that you can take control of specific automatic processes. Your beating heart is another autonomic process controlled by the hypothalamus, but we know that if we deliberately relax or meditate we can slow the normal heart rate down. It is possible to control the heart even under stressful conditions as I have had a major hernia operation without any anaesthetic, no general, and no local. I did not do this through hypnosis; I did it by controlling my thoughts. I know I can do this, and so did the surgical staff who performed the operation. There is nothing clever or magic about me. If I can do it anyone can do it, with the right training.

So you can interfere with or control specific autonomic processes of the body. Thinking is an autonomic process as it is controlled by the hypothalamus. I have found the process of controlling my negative thoughts, (thoughts which are detrimental to my health) a very useful tool in reducing, and eliminating issues from my past, which trapped me in unwanted behaviour. I call this the Dynamic Thought Transfer process or DTT for short.

Current understanding is that in an adult, 99% of thoughts are a product of past learned experiences, in other words they originate from the sub-conscious, from memory. The older you get the more you rely on your memory to guide you in your behaviour. Remember that your thoughts are only your interpretation of the internal/external environmental signals received by you, mixed with other environmental signals previously received. Your behaviour is created by you, and this behaviour is 'visible' to you through your thoughts. Your body does not perform any function unless you authorise it to do so. All your behaviour is influenced by your thoughts, therefore it is necessary to be able to identify those thoughts which have a detrimental effect on your health ... what I term as negative thoughts.

This is a description of what I do.

I verbalise the following words. I may say them aloud or mumble them, but when you first start doing this process it is essential to verbalise, and not to try and consciously think a thought to control another thought. You need to develop new learning behaviour, and the best way I have found to do this is to verbalise the words, (say the words with your voice).

So when a negative thought creeps into my consciousness I say;

"Stop."

"I don't want that thought."

"Take it away and move it into Trash."

"Do that now."

As I say the words "Do that now", I move my eyes from one side of my face to the other in a sweeping movement. It does not matter if you move your eyes right to left or left to right; it is the eye movement that is important.

Could it be that the reason this process works is because every moment of the day you are allowing your body to automatically record your memories into your sub-conscious with the emotions you are attaching to your thoughts and actions. Your body creates a file in your sub-conscious matching your emotion. This is an autonomic process controlled by the hypothalamus, and it is an evolved gift giving us the ability to record and recall (memory) elements of our life. The development of memory has been a primary catalyst in the development of many life-forms. We can *'interfere'* with this autonomic process. The fact that we can do this may imply that our evolution, in human form, has deliberately provided this ability, to enable 'software updates' to our memories and behaviour in order that adaptation and change can be within the life-form control, and not totally an environmental or genetic trigger?

Verbalizing the word *"Stop."* inhibits the hypothalamus from producing the peptide.

Verbalizing the words, *"I don't want that thought."* Informs the sub-conscious that you do not want that thought therefore it will start to move the thought back to where it came from.

So immediately you verbalize the words, *"Take it away and move it into Trash"*, your sub-conscious will create a file called 'Trash', and move the offending thought into that file. As there is no emotion attached to the 'Trash' file, any emotion attached to your negative thought will be disconnected, and the thought in 'Trash' will have no emotion to trigger any emotional behaviour.

Verbalizing the words *"Do that now"*, and moving your eyes seems to be the catalyst that gives this simple process the power, as it gives a firm definitive instruction to your body of what you want it to do, and it does it every time, all the time. Remember, your body only obeys the instructions that you give it either consciously or sub-consciously through your belief system.

If you have a negative feeling, and you don't know what the thought is that has triggered the feeling, then use the same process, but change the words slightly. Say the following words.

"Stop"

"I don't know what it is, but I don't want it."

"Take it away and move it into Trash."

"Do that now." *(move your eyes)*

Do not let your current belief system stop you from trying this process. It works. What can happen when you move a negative thought or feeling, your sub-conscious can immediately bring you another similar thought or feeling, because your sub-conscious is there to protect you, and it still responds to the signals it is receiving. It has no judgement or free-will, it only responds to the signals in your environment or your created thoughts. You might think *'this is the same thought I've just had; the process does not work'*. This would be an incorrect assumption.

Immediately you move one negative thought your sub-conscious is going to keep trying to protect you with your old belief system behaviour, so it will immediately bring you another thought or feeling (memory instruction) that matches the signals it is receiving. What you must understand is that current scientific understanding is that the hypothalamus can produce over one hundred thousand different peptides. Your hypothalamus can produce a peptide to match your strength of emotion, equivalent to many decimal places. You might recognise the actual thought, but you would never distinguish between the different strengths of emotion chemically imprinted in the released peptide. So once you move your thought to trash, your sub-conscious will bring you another (similar) thought ... it will have a different strength of emotion attached to it, and therefore you should move it into trash using the same technique.

If you think ... *"This is the same thought, or this does not work,"* ... then this is a negative thought ... move it to trash. Remember you are currently thinking with your old belief system, which might make you skeptical of the process.

Amber is a gold-coloured substance formed from the fossilized resin or sap of ancient trees. Amber only forms when the sap gets trapped in the earth, subjected to great pressures and timescales of millions of years. Most amber is between thirty and one hundred million years old dating back to the Cretaceous Period when dinosaurs dominated the earth. Many small animals have been found trapped in amber; preserved and stuck forever. Your belief system can trap you in ancient thinking, your belief system can trap you in the past, (in amber) if you let it. Learn how to release yourself.

You can delete all the negative thoughts you have moved into your 'Trash' file at any time. The process is as follows. Again you verbalise the words.

"Delete the contents of my trash file ... Do that now" (move your eyes).

To stop your sub-conscious from bringing you negative destructive thoughts, then all you have to do is change the environmental signals you are receiving. To do this you can move around, sit in another chair, or my favorite, dance and turn around (spinning slowly). Your sub-conscious has to protect you, so it can only bring you conscious thoughts from the signals it is receiving. If the signals are from an unknown event or a neutral event, then it will respond accordingly, and so will your peptides.

Do not allow your current belief system to stop you from trying this process. Do not become selective in what you move. If the thought or feeling is negative (detrimental to your health) then move it into 'Trash'. I have a saying ... *'If in doubt move it out'*. Practice this process for three months, after which if you want to stop doing it, then do so ... I would bet that you continue using the technique for the rest of your life.

STEP SIX: INVEST IN YOURSELF EVERYDAY OF YOUR LIFE.

You write your destiny in your thoughts and deeds on the pages of this moment. You need to cut the strings from that which ties you to the past, and invest in your dreams. Remember that it is only you who has labeled your experiences good or bad, black or white. Whatever you have experienced, it is only an experience. Do not label any experience, for then it has room to grow; you feed it with your judgmental reflections. What matters is now ... this moment. Make this moment part of your dream; do not build your life on what has been, but on what can be.

How do you know what you need to know? People are working in industries today that did not exist ten to fifteen years ago. Many students starting University are learning 'stuff' that will be obsolete before they leave. You can only learn in this moment what is; your life is potential. How will you know your potential? By knowing what is. Try and have an understanding of as much knowledge as you can; for then you will be able to link current knowledge in a new way.

That is evolution, and evolution is potential in this moment. Invest your time, your energy, and your senses to understanding who and what you are. Take from experiences the knowledge that you are creating your life, now, in human form, on Planet Earth. Life should be lived on purpose, passionately; always seek to fulfill a passion. If you are cleaning the streets to earn a living, then be the best street cleaner you can be. Whatever you do ... do it with love and peace in your heart, and with gratitude for your time, now, in human form, on Planet Earth. Always be the best you can be with what you have got now, for that is all you can be in this moment.

Consider the possibility that following these six steps will significantly enhance your life. Why would you ever desire to stop doing them on a daily basis for the rest of your life? It is not the truth, but the best guess or understanding that science, philosophy, medicine, and religion all over the Planet have at this moment in time, and that is, that the greatest power on the Planet is love. You cannot truly love someone or something else, unless you love yourself. You cannot give what you have not got.

To love yourself you need to know that you are responsible for your life, so live your life with a passion, love whatever you ask your body and mind to do. Treat your body with respect, and learn how to maintain it to the best advantage. There is significant evidence that this can be achieved through meditation, eliminating negative thoughts, setting and following loving and healthy intentions, and creating a mind-set for each day. This can only be done by you, no one other than you can do this for your body and mind; it is all down to you to invest in knowledge and understanding.

... would you ask someone to eat a meal for you to satisfy your hunger? ...

... knowledge is not something you can give or receive; it is a practice, self inflicted, and visible only through wisdom ...

Trapped in Amber

Trapped in Amber

Be aware of your emotions while reading the narrative.

WHAT IS CONSCIOUSNESS?

The following is a new and personal theory of consciousness; I ask you to read the narrative without judgement. If you find yourself disagreeing or agreeing with the theory then please move that thought. Remember that forming an opinion or judgement limits your ability, as it confines your thinking into a predetermined space of right or wrong, black or white. If you must assume a stance then use the neutral thought of *'interesting'* as the hook for your feelings. Let the words sink into your sub-conscious and leave them there under the heading of interesting. Then as you go through life, events will happen that will allow you to test out the theory for yourself. You will then form your own view on the subject. Please remember I do not want you to believe anything ... I want you to know it.

Consciousness is one of the big questions at the beginning of the 21st Century. Some scientists speculate that consciousness is a human function, or it may exist in other life-forms, but it is nonetheless a phenomenon of the brain. In other words consciousness is a function of how the brain works. They refer to the microtubules as being a connection to consciousness.

Other scientists talk about consciousness being inherent in the Universe; they refer to the matrix of consciousness talking about a conscious Universe. This theory is generated through the work of quantum mechanics, which is providing new ways to view and experience the Universe through rigorous mathematical formula and experimentation. There is no consensus of opinion at the present time, as to how these theories affect the view that only human life-forms possess consciousness.

Resolving challenging problems is all about asking the right questions. If you think consciousness is a function of the brain then you will ask questions only about the brain. If you think consciousness is only specific to certain life-forms, then you will limit your questions and search to life-forms that fit a defined criteria. Let me share with you the questions I asked, and the observations and experiences I had, that brought me to the Lucy Theory of Consciousness. Please understand that this is my theoretical explanation, and it is not a main stream scientific view. It is my interpretation of my understanding of my current knowledge. I have changed and developed my ideas over the last eighteen months as new knowledge has come into my understanding; I hope that I continue to have the freedom of mind to continue changing and growing. It is new thinking, challenging and controversial.

I started with the first question; 'What is consciousness?' From this initial question I asked myself four more questions.

1. What are humans made from? Answer: Atoms.
2. What are other living entities made from? Answer: Atoms.
3. What is the Universe made from? Answer: Atoms.
4. Is there anything made from anything other than atoms? Answer: No.

I do not propose that consciousness is an evolved process, therefore, the starting point for all enquiries on consciousness must be associated with atoms and/or their constituent parts.

What is the current definition of consciousness? There are many, here are some;

1. An alert cognitive state in which you are aware of yourself and your situation.
2. Consciousness is said to be the process of a thinker focusing the thought of some aspect of existence.
3. It is the ability to generalize a small object into a larger object or collection of objects.
4. The capacity to visualize things in the mind before they occur in the real world.
5. Consciousness is the ability to sense time.

6. Only conscious entities have a sense of self or collective identity.

7. Awareness or concern for a particular issue or situation. The immediate knowledge or perception of the presence of any object, state, or sensation.

8. Consciousness is a quality of mind enabling subjectivity, self-awareness, sentience, sapience, ability to perceive relationships between self and environment.

9. Consciousness is strongly associated with an awakened state.

I asked the question: Are these definitions biased to the human race? Clearly they are, in that it would need a human to decide if another creature was conscious. This means humans take control of whether something has consciousness or not. This is power; power is control; control limits knowledge. So I decided to define consciousness as:

Consciousness is the subject that enables perception of objective stimuli.

For example what this means is that any entity is conscious if it can act on internal and external objective stimuli. Example, can it distinguish light from dark, can it detect food or danger? Does it have the ability to interpret its environment? If it can then it is conscious.

It is the Lucy Theory that consciousness is consciousness. Consciousness is constant and available; access to it is through the brain. The life-form's ability to function in the environment is not down to consciousness, but to the complexity of the brain, and the evolution of the life-form. For example current knowledge says that a typical adult human is conscious forty times per second. The snail is conscious much less ... other creatures may be conscious more or less than humans, we have not got the understanding at this moment. What is clear is that the rate of consciousness (state of consciousness) is dependent upon how well the brain functions. It is a consequence of the complexity of the brain, not a function within the brain.

The words 'life-form' denote all living entities on the Planet that have a cellular structure which includes DNA (deoxyribonucleic acid) and/or RNA (ribonucleic acid). This includes both prokaryotic and eukaryotic cells.

It could be suggested that consciousness is connected to physical movement of the life-form. Physical movement in living forms would appear to be connected to chemicals and electromagnetic pulses known as electricity. The Lucy Theory is proposing that consciousness has nothing to do with movement or electromagnetic pulses, but is a result of a discrete *'charge'* of energy.

What is the difference between electricity and charge in a life-form?

A DESCRIPTION OF ELECTRICITY WITHIN THE LIFE-FORM:

It is accepted by all biologists that the best guess or understanding we have at this moment is that everything life-forms do, is controlled and enabled by chemical and electrical signals. Chemical interaction is part of the life-form's function; however, the chemicals are controlled by electrical signals. Electricity is the key to the survival of all life-forms. Electrical signals allow for almost instantaneous response to chemically controlled messages. Almost all of our cells are capable of producing electricity. Negativity is the natural state of the human cell. It is the imbalance between potassium and sodium ions inside and outside the cell that sets up the capacity to produce electricity.

The cell membranes perform a process called the sodium-potassium gate. At rest your cells have more potassium ions inside than sodium ions; there are more sodium ions outside the cell. At a resting position there is not enough movement to generate electricity. When the body needs to send messages from point 'A' to point 'B', due to a chemical signal, it opens the membrane gate. When opened, sodium and potassium ions move freely into and out of the cell. Potassium ions leave the cell attracted to the outside of the membrane. The sodium charged ions move the other way into the cell. The result is a switch in the concentrations of the two types of ions. This flip between the ions generates an electromagnetic pulse, which has been influenced by a chemical marker.

It is these electromagnetic pulses that tell the organs of the life-form what to do. When scientists talk about the nervous system sending signals to the brain, or synapses firing, or the brain telling your hands to pick up a sandwich; what is actually happening is electrical signals are passing between point 'A' and point 'B' in the body. There is not a wire connecting things together in the body; electrical signals are passed cell to cell until it reaches its destination, utilising the nervous system of the life-form. These signals move chemicals within the life-form, and are triggered by chemical interaction. Electricity requires an outside source of fuel, and is a movement of energy from point 'A' to point 'Z'.

Electricity in the life-form is the electromagnetic signal created when cell movement disturbs the sodium and potassium ions, and this reaction creates an electrical pulse. The life-form only has consciousness if enough electric pulses can be generated to maintain functions within the life-form, because there is a dual purpose to producing electricity in the life-form, and that is to signal movement, and to convert food into energy.

Trapped in Amber

A DESCRIPTION OF CHARGE.

Now it is understood that the speed of sound is a basic property of the atmosphere that changes with temperature. For a given set of conditions, the speed of sound defines the velocity at which sound waves travel through a substance, such as air. Based on the standard atmospheric model this value has been defined as; 1,116.4 feet per second, 340.3 meters per second, 761.2 miles per hour, 1,225.1 kilometers per hour, or 661.5 knots.

So sound waves are waves of sound in air. What are light waves a wave in?

Let me try and explain the challenge in another way. If you took a glass container, inside of which you placed an old fashioned alarm clock with a visible bell and hammer alarm mechanism that was constantly ringing. If you then sealed the container, and extracted all the air, thus creating a vacuum inside the glass container, you would not be able to hear the alarm clock ringing because sound only travels through air, and as there is no air in the container, no sound would be heard. You would be able to see the hammer hitting the bell mechanism, but you would not hear any sound. That is relatively simple to understand, however, you can still see the clock. To see something, your eyes have to detect light. We understand that light is a wave. That means that light waves are being emitted through the vacuum, so what are the light waves travelling through? The clock is in a vacuum, a vacuum is suppose to have nothing inside of it. We know it is not air ... what is it?

What follows is a little bit of Quantum Physics, even the scientists who support and demonstrate what I am about to explain are challenged by it. Do not allow your belief system to create negative labels to block you from reading about this amazing process. The information is the best knowledge and understanding that rigorous experimentation has provided.

It is Carl Heisenberg's Uncertainty Principle that states at a very fundamental level of the Universe, nature is based on uncertainty. At the quantum level you can measure where something is, but you would lose precise information about the speed of the object. Or you can measure its speed, but you would lose precise information relating to where it was. In other words you could know precisely how fast something was travelling, but you would not be able to determine precisely its position.

Heisenberg's mathematics show that this bizarre relationship is an inescapable feature at the quantum scale, and relates to other quantities of measurements, like time and energy. For example, if you were able to examine a small space inside a vacuum, then you could determine precisely the amount of energy within the space. However, if you were able to slow time down, then things start becoming very strange. The

Heisenberg Principle shows that because you have slowed time down, and stretched it out, you have lost the precise information of how much energy is in the space. If you slow time down even further, then Heisenberg suggests that you would be so uncertain about how much energy is inside of the space, there is a chance that there is so much energy, it could literally create new particles from nothing; providing that the new particles disappeared as quickly as they came. This process of creating particles of matter, ('electrons'), would borrow energy from the vacuum and pop into existence. Also at the same time an anti-electron (anti-matter) would appear, and if the electron and anti-electron collided, they would annihilate themselves turning their mass into energy. Trillions of these actions would be going on in very, very small spaces, and in very, very short time intervals. This strange action is called 'quantum fluctuations' and results in a 'charge', a discrete package of energy.

I know this seems incredible, but read on.
Heisenberg is suggesting that in very, very small amounts of time and space, something could come from nothing. A small package of energy is created from nothing, caused by the collision of the electron and anti-electron (matter and anti-matter). This is now establishing a new understanding of how the initial Universe was created.

It is suggested that the Universe was created from quantum fluctuations, which created a void (a vacuum) by inflation caused by the energy created (*the charge*) from the interaction of matter and anti-matter. The void was not empty, but teeming with trillions of other quantum fluctuations. For example, in one drop of water there are literally billions of quantum fluctuations going on all the time. In fact in every atom, billions of quantum fluctuations are going on all the time.

The particles created by these fluctuations have become known as *'virtual particles'*. As each piece of matter pops into existence it immediately pops out again as it collides with some anti-matter annihilating itself, fueling the expansion of the vacuum. However, it is suggested that one electron (matter) in every billion did not get destroyed, or disappear, and that provided the matter (mass) that has created the stars, planets and galaxies of the Universe. These small pieces of matter also went on to create all life.

So over time, the void expanded, due to the energy created through collision, and the electrons that survived created mass. The stars, planets, and galaxies are not separated from the vacuum (the void), but are part of the void. When we talk about the Universe expanding, it is not the galaxies that are expanding or moving away from Planet Earth, it is the void, the space between the galaxies. As the void expands (inflates) it carries the galaxies meshed in the matrix of the void with it. The stars and planets are trapped in the galaxies though the power of gravity. It is the vacuum of Space that is expanding. All the matter in the Universe is part of the vacuum of Space, including you, including consciousness. A vacuum is the Universe's default state.

Everywhere including the vacuum of Space is alive with quantum fluctuations, which are little packages of energy which appear, and very quickly disappear. This is allowable because of the Heisenberg Uncertainty Principle, which shows that you can borrow energy from nothing, as long as you pay it back quickly. This has now been evidenced in laboratories from work done by Willis Lamb as shown in the BBC 4 documentary with Jim Al-Khalili, Everything and Nothing, March 2011. Rigorous tests have shown that these fluctuations exist in a vacuum, and the mathematics of Paul Dirac, which provide the calculations to assess how much electrons would be affected by virtual particles, has been proven to be correct up to one part in a million, after experimentation. This is strong evidence, providing an accurate and powerful description of reality. It also provides an explanation of why electrons 'orbiting' an atom, appear and then disappear, reappearing in a different place without seemingly going through the intervening space. It is the process of quantum fluctuation. Nothingness cannot exist in nature.

Trapped in Amber

The understanding gained from this knowledge allows, for the first time, a bridge to connect the Special Theory of Relativity by Einstein, which describes things close to the speed of light, and Planck's Theory of Quantum Mechanics, which sets rules for the very, very small.

Every atom is 99.99% vacuum. Virtual particles are literally popping into and out of existence all the time. We are living in an ocean that is alive with virtual fluctuations that are constantly creating a 'charge of pure energy'.

It is accepted that energy cannot be destroyed only changed. When a virtual particle comes into existence, borrowing energy from the vacuum, and then disappears, where does the energy go? We know with some certainty, that these actions are going on trillions of times, all the time, within every square centimeter, everywhere in the Universe. The Lucy Theory is proposing that consciousness is the *'charge'* created by the virtual particle when it appears and then disappears.

Quantum reality has shaped the structure of the Universe; our world is the quantum world, the difference is that our world has been inflated many times. Everything came from the vacuum created by one particle appearing from nothing, creating energy (*a charge*) when colliding with anti-matter. Thus setting off a chain reaction of quantum fluctuations, and from that seed, grew our Universe and all life.

The conscious *'charge'* drives the life-form, using the brain to provide a subjective state of being, enabling perception of objective stimuli. If the brain is damaged or under the influence of drugs, then the brain's ability to respond to consciousness will be altered, not consciousness. Consciousness is not social, it has no boundary. The brain's complexity allows consciousness to be a conduit, allowing the life-form to interpret signals creating a view of the environment. Consciousness does not grow old; we have the same consciousness charge now as when we were children. Consciousness is a constant. Consciousness is not intelligence; it is the ocean in which everything swims, enabling life-forms with brain processes to experience stimuli, allowing the brain to inform the life-form.

Consciousness is a constant 'charge'. There is no power to stop this process or to improve this process; it simply is. Electricity is on demand, and will happen if certain conditions are met, which can be pre-determined. Electricity needs to be informed (fueled) before it can be created. Consciousness is non-computable and cannot be pre-determined. Electricity needs to be fueled and flows from one point to another, the collision of matter and anti-matter, *'charge'* does not flow.

An analogy to help understand this relationship of consciousness with electricity would be a driver, and the car they drive. The car relates to the cells of the body, which produce electricity when fuel is applied. If the parts of the car could signal to each other through their mechanical and electrical circuits they would signal ready to go. It cannot switch itself on or move; for that it needs the driver, and that is consciousness. The two powers are correlated; for cells to work effectively they need to make electricity, for that they need fuel (food), but to make electricity they need consciousness to drive the life-form. It only works if the two sources cooperate.

Without consciousness cells cannot create electricity, movement or function. The creation of electromagnetic pulses in the life-form is not magic, it does not just occur because cells exist. The electromagnetic pulse is enabled because of the presence of consciousness. The Theory proposes that the 'spark' from the energy created by the disappearing virtual particle, triggers the heart cell to beat in the zygote cells, twelve to fourteen days after conception. This actual event has never been explained by anyone; how one cell knows that it has to become the heart, and start beating, is still a mystery, but perhaps the process of where the energy comes from to start the heart can now be explained.

LET US LOOK CLOSER AT THE BRAIN.
When you look at an event, person or thing, does your brain show you the correct picture of what you are looking at?

You may be nodding your head and saying "Of course it does." So perhaps you will look at the diagram below, and in your mind describe what you see.

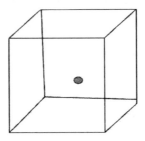

You would probably describe the diagram as a cube with a dot in the cube. On which face of the cube do you see the dot. Do you see it on the front face of the cube that is slightly facing to your left? Or do you see the dot on the front face of the cube slightly facing your right?

Close your eyes for five seconds, then open your eyes and focus your attention on the dot. When you see the cube change shape raise your right hand.

What is happening? How can the cube move on the page? How can the cube change shape while you are looking at it? The answer is that when you see the dot to your left you are seeing it through your right brain; when you see it to your right you are seeing it through your left brain.

Can you control which side of the brain you see it through? Can you control which cube shape you see? Can you see both shapes at the same time? Can you feel anything when the left brain switches to the right brain? No you cannot, which proves definitively that you cannot be sure that what you think you see, is what actually is there. How do you know which side of your brain is creating the picture in your head at any one time? You are walking through life believing the pictures that your brain produces, but how will you know when your brain switches your perception of what is there? You now understand the difference between believing, and the need for you to know.

The brain is an electrochemical organ using electromagnetic energy to function. The electricity coming from the brain can be measured in brainwave activity. There are four categories of brainwave activity and all humans experience the same characteristic brainwaves. There are different interpretations of this data.

1. Beta: 12 to 38 cycles per second; this is fully awake, fully aware, concentration, logical thinking, and active

conversation. The range of brain cycles within beta would determine intensity of action.

2. Alpha: 8 to 12 cycles per second; relaxation, non-arousal, slight meditation.

3. Theta: 3 to 8 cycles per second; day dreaming, dreaming, creativity, meditation, out of body experiences.

4. Delta: 3 to 1.5 or less cycles per second; deep dreamless sleep.

The accepted scientific work on brainwaves, implies that the speed of forty times a second consciousness, associated with the waking state of a human, would vary in meditation. The Lucy Theory rejects this statement. It does not mean that consciousness slows down due to meditation; consciousness is constant; it is the brain that slows down, controlling the life-form within the boundaries of its ability. It is recognised that the waking human brain is possibly conscious forty times per second. This may not be the limit of consciousness; it is only the limit of the human brain, whilst in a waking state. (Best guess or understanding at this moment.) When a life-form meditates, the brain changes; I would propose expands in consciousness, by letting go of some of the life-form controls. It is the functioning of the brain, which alters under meditation, not the functioning of consciousness.

You can test this with anyone, and the results are the same every time. There is much written about meditation improving a person's perceptions and consciousness. Creativity and health implications are often cited as specific consequences.

The Lucy Theory proposes that consciousness is not a function of the brain itself. A complex brain with the use of good external sensing, could evolve complexity to provide the life-form with a record and replay feature (memory), that would facilitate learning, and therefore give rise to made-up (local/unique to the life-form) experiences, which would then instruct the life-form, allowing it to create an illusionary world view. This would provide a competitive edge relating to survival.

Consciousness does not contribute to subjectivity relating to the interpretation of experiences that is down to the independent life-form's interpretation of environmental signals. Consciousness has no belief ... the belief system is part of the human condition, (and other life-forms also). The labeling of experiences is the product of learned behaviour. This is a subjective action enabled by consciousness, not determined by consciousness. The different *'strengths'* of consciousness are determined by the brain within the life-form, not by the 'conscious charge', which is always constant. Consciousness does not contribute to survival as it is infinite.

Summary:

Gravity holds galaxies together, electromagnetism is the force that would theoretically rip a nucleus apart, the weak nuclear force governs radioactivity, and the strong nuclear force is the force that holds a nucleus together. These are four fundamental principles of the Universe. I am postulating that consciousness could be a fundamental principle of the Universe, and is a product of the virtual particle hypothesis that suggests that a vacuum is alive with pure energy, and under discrete situations, creates consciousness that empowers independent life-forms. It may also be connected to why life-forms grow in size over time.

There are three basic states of a life-form, waking, sleep, and coma, these are elements of qualia, and at this moment we do not know the minimum size of brain capacity that would be needed to experience consciousness. Current research implies that the vacuum in all atoms, is teeming with billions of virtual particles, and it is now accepted understanding that a *'vacuum'*, the place where we consider nothing to be, has in fact got structure. It is this structure (the virtual particle activity) that bends light throughout the Universe. The Lucy Theory proposes that consciousness is in the vacuum of the Universal ocean of virtual particles. Everything is touched by consciousness, however it is only reflected by life-forms with appropriate brain capacity.

... consciousness has no belief ...
the belief system is part of the
human condition ...

Trapped in Amber

Trapped in Amber

Be aware of your emotions while reading the narrative.

WHAT IS QUALIA AND HAVE YOU GOT FREE-WILL?

Consider for a moment that you are in the high street of a busy town. You can smell freshly baked bread as you pass the bakers shop. There are traffic noises filling the air. You can smell coffee as you pass the local cafe. The experiences that you are having as you walk down the high street are your private judgments of the world around you. They are your conscious/sub-conscious values and labels that allow you to make sense of your environment. These private experiences have a quality all of their own, and in philosophy they are known as *'qualia'*.

Experiences are all unique to the 'experiencer'. We personalize every moment giving some moments more relevance or value than others. How do we do this? Candice Pert, (1997) and Bruce Lipton (2005, 2009) are two biologists that have laid the foundation for acceptance that when we attach a value or meaning to a thought the hypothalamus in the brain produces a peptide. As already explained, the cell, if influenced by the peptide, can change the behaviour of the cell.

Our cells are influenced (changed) by the value or meaning we give to our thoughts; these we call emotions. The emotion is a product of our learned behaviour, and it is this learned behaviour (emotion), which instructs the hypothalamus to produce a matching peptide.

For clarity I am going to repeat some things expressed before, in order to put to you my theory. When I was born I had no memories that I could associate with to make sense of the world. I was in a trance for approximately the first six months of my life. I did not recognise or have the ability to use memories inherited through my parents. As I grew I started to experience through my senses, the signals that coloured my world view. I began attaching meaning or value to my experiences. Many of these were patterns and behaviours from my parents, but some were my own baby interpretations. These attached meanings or values, triggered the hypothalamus in my brain to make peptides to match my selected meaning or value.

These experiences were filed in my subconscious under the relevant peptide (meaning or value) heading. My subconscious became my memory. Memory is a process that has evolved to protect us. Memory allows us to record an experience with an appropriate meaning or value so that if it occurs again we would not have to go through the whole thinking process working out what to do. This was to stop us being eaten or killed. Learning can only take place if there is a method of recording and replaying. We have evolved a process called memory which allows us to record and replay. This is made possible through the relationship of the senses and the hypothalamus peptide.

When like experiences or similar experiences occur, my memory triggers my hypothalamus to produce the recorded peptide, and my body reacts the way I taught it to react from past experience(s). This is an on-going process, consequently if I record an early experience(s) with negative meaning, and nothing happens to change my meaning, and I keep reinforcing that view, then that memory will become behaviour. The hypothalamus can make different strengths of peptide; almost the equivalent to making different strengths of peptide to many decimal places. So an experience can have a peptide called fear attached to it at strength of 1.1234 and another experience with fear attached at strength of 10.3456.

These recorded memories will reinforce behaviour for similar environmental signals received in the future. My thoughts that trigger the 'fear' may appear to me to be the same thoughts; however the different thoughts could have different strengths of emotion making them unique thoughts. A thought without an emotion (meaning or value) attached does not become a memory. To make something a memory you have to 'hook it' with a label.

Recognition is a memory. Looking in the mirror and recognising self is not connected at all with consciousness, it is a function of memory, and a learned behaviour. Without memory it would not be possible to recognise anyone or anything. That includes you. Recognising self is a response to a learned memory, hooked by a peptide. The Lucy Theory strongly suggests that any 'life-form' that does not possess a memory or has not developed a strong enough memory would not recognise self. It has nothing to do with consciousness.

We teach ourselves through the action of our thought process, by ascribing various positive or negative values or meanings to our experience(s). In other words we are teaching ourselves qualia. Free-will unfolds within the boundaries of our belief system.

Qualia is not a thing, it is not a function in the 'life-form' body, it is not something magic that makes humans different from other creatures; qualia is a learning process that is available in all living things. How can this be evidenced?

Evidence of learned qualia in humans:

Many years ago I worked for an industrial organisation that
went into receivership. I was retained by the administrator of
the bankrupt company to help sort out the affairs in order to
try and sell the organisation to a new owner. One of my sad
duties was to make many people redundant; a fate I knew
would eventually be mine. I was directed by the accountant,
who was appointed by the bank, I had to read ... word for
word ... a notice that was prepared for me, to all the people
who would lose their jobs. I was instructed that I was not to
say anything other than the words on the notice. Each person
was to be given a copy, and then they had to leave the
premises.

I had four managers reporting to me, and could only retain
two. It was a difficult time in my life, but I made the
decision who was to be retained, and I called into my office
the first manager who was to be made redundant. He had
worked in the company for just over two years. I was seated
at my desk and he sat down facing me. I explained what I
had been instructed to do, and with obvious sadness I read
out the notice. When I had finished, the manager stood up,
walked around the side of my desk; I thought he was coming
to shake my hand so I stood up. He hit me, and I fell back
into my chair; he swore and was clearly upset and angry. My
secretary rushed in, and was able to usher the man out of the
office, he was still using abusive and aggressive language.

After cleaning myself up, I had to see my next manager who had arrived at my office at the appointed time. Now this man had been with the company for over twenty years, he was very well respected and over six feet tall. I explained what I had been instructed to do, and with obvious sadness I read out the notice. When I had finished the manager stood up, walked around the side of my desk. You can only imagine what was going through my mind ... my secretary hovered in the doorway. This man towered over my 1.7 metres frame, he held out both arms and pulled me towards him and embraced me. There were tears in his eyes as he said "Thank you ... I know this must have been very hard for you. You have been a great boss to work for, and I am not afraid of making changes in my life. It will be an exciting and challenging time, but I know the situation is not your fault, and my life is my responsibility."

I openly admit there were tears in my eyes as this wonderful huge man pressed my face into his chest. He shook my hand and left the company where he had worked for the last twenty years.

Both men had been in the same environment, my office; both men had heard exactly the same words. The reaction from the men had been very different ... why? You do not have to think what you think. You think what you think, and attach meaning or value to your thoughts because of the meanings you attached to past experiences. You teach yourself by creating your own behaviour. Your thoughts are framed within the boundaries of your belief system. Qualia is not a thing, it is an interpretation of an experience coloured by a peptide. It is a learned response to an experience. The sunrise or sunset can be a beautiful experience to some, but can mean danger or abuse to others.

The reason why qualia is a personal process is because it is a personal interpretation of an experience reinforced by a personalized peptide, mixed into a memory bank of other experiences tagged with peptides. No two 'life-forms' can have identical memories, there will always be a difference no matter how small.

The neurons in the human brain number over one hundred billion; each one can connect to between ten thousand and fifty thousand other neurons sending and receiving messages from the senses to coordinate the actions of the person. Of the three main types of neuron; sensory, interneuron, and motor neuron; biologists now understand that the neurons found in the human brain are identical to the neurons found in the brain of all other living creatures. It is the quantity of neurons in the brain that differentiates life-forms.

One neuron has no measurable impact on activity or behaviour; put one hundred billion together in a small space, and let them communicate at super-speed with ten thousand to fifty thousand other neurons; now you have a complex organism with complex changeable behaviour. The states of consciousness (waking, sleeping, coma) are qualia controlled by the brain; consciousness is an enabler of being, is constant, and needs a state of brain function to access it. A life-form still has consciousness even if in a coma, but in the coma state (the brain) denies access to some body responses.

Evidence of learned qualia in plants:

Plants can discern sense of self, by identifying sunlight as not being part of it. Therefore the plant has consciousness.

Summary:

Qualia is taught and is part of learned behaviour, (a record and recall facility) it is not a function within the body, nor is it a function of consciousness. We have not got free-will, we only have choices based on our learned behaviour, (belief system), and only that which we can record and recall. You will not do what your behaviour inhibits you to do, so there is no free-will, only learned responses within boundaries.

It is choice (learned behaviour), not circumstance that determines actions.

... free-will unfolds only within the boundaries of our belief system ...

Trapped in Amber

Trapped in Amber

Be aware of your emotions while reading the narrative.

WHY CAN WE NOT BE CONSCIOUSLY AWARE OF WHAT IT IS LIKE TO BE SOMEONE ELSE?

The reason why this is not possible is simply that the cellular life-form (the person, animal, insect, plant, bacteria, cell) can only have a representation of the world from the environmental signals the individual life-form receives. And then, even if the life-form received the same environmental signals as others, it could not have exactly the same view as another life-form, unless it interpreted all previous environmental signals in the same way, creating the same peptides (emotions). Even identical twins have some differences as it is not possible to make one hundred billion neurons fire in the same way in two different life-forms.

Consciousness is not a thing in the brain, it is a fundamental principle of the Universe that has enabled certain life-forms' to evolve record, store, and recall memory, which has enabled learned behaviour. We have not got free-will ... we have got choices depending upon our learned behaviour patterns. The choices are local to the individual person or life-form. A client came to me because she was afraid of flying. She had never flown before so she had never had the experience of flying. Her belief system inhibited her from having the experience. Why? *The diagrams 'How Behaviour is Created' page 97' and 'How the Belief System is Formed' page 108 reproduced earlier will remind you.*

Remember the individual will relate to the internal/external environment through the interpretation of the signals from their senses; how the individual interprets the signals, will create the belief system. These signals received by the brain, inform the belief system through the application of attaching peptides to the interpretations of the signals, (interpretations are thoughts). The values or meanings (emotions) attached to the thought is recorded into memory, under the heading of the value or meaning, (emotion). This creates the belief system and becomes behaviour.

The belief system will enable what is recorded in memory to be the life-forms view of how to behave, determining what experiences they will comfortably have. The experiences of the life-form reinforce the belief system, the product of which is the personality and behaviour of the form. This then determines the world view of the life-form, and what they will attract into their lives. This completes the circle and the life-form lives life stuck in the belief system that they have created. The 'cause' is the external environment and the 'effect' is the personality and behaviour. Experiences are not the driver for personality and behaviour, they are only a conduit. The drivers of the belief system are the senses of the life-form.

When something happens to trigger one or more of the external senses of the life-form, the brain communicates with all the cells in the body what is going on. Biologists suggest that our brain can handle external and internal signals at over four hundred billion bits per second. The memories stored in the cells, are triggered by the external signals coming into the brain, and if they have a learned response to the external signals, (something that the life-form has experienced before or similar to something experienced before) then the cells will communicate with the brain.

The brain will now instruct the hypothalamus to trigger peptides to match the learned behaviour remembered by the cells. The peptides will flood the life-form body, and the life-form will automatically respond to the learned behaviour from the past. We constantly repeat what we have learned from the past. I would suggest that we constantly live in our past memories, constantly reinforcing our behaviour. The reason is clear; not to do so would mean having to think about what to do every moment of the day. Can you imagine existence without memory?

The brain is not the store of memory, the cells are. The brain is the receiver and transmitter of the life-form, and if damaged, then this will result in loss of communication to the appropriate structures throughout the life-form. Take the case of a life-form (human person) falling and hitting their head, damaging their brain. The result of the fall is the person can no longer move their left arm. This does not mean that the left arm is damaged. What it means is that the communication system between the part of the brain that communicates with the left arm is damaged.

The same applies to memory. If the part of the brain associated with communicating with the cells regarding memory (either long term or short term) is damaged, then communication with the cells is no longer possible. It is about communication, and should not infer that memory is in the brain. The Lucy Theory supports the premise that the brain is not a store, but is a very powerful transmitter and receiver of signals from external and internal sources. Consciousness is the operating system, the brain is the source of the programme files, and the organs of the body are the software sub-routines linked to the programme files, (the brain). Life needs both an operating system (consciousness) and programmes (organs or organelle functions); they are interdependent and inseparable because consciousness is the subject that enables perception of objective stimuli using the brain functions of the life-form.

The way to change the belief system is to change what your body senses; for these influences will automatically change the belief system, (the programme files) enabling new experiences or beliefs to be engaged. I have been putting this principle into practice in my Psychotherapy work since 2004, collecting data on clients to verify that understanding this process, and knowing how to control it, is the basis for significant benefits which are helping people stop their negative thinking, allowing them to make different choices, thus changing the outcomes in their lives.

Summary:

Consciousness is the operating system that enables life-forms with a brain function to perceive objective stimuli. (This may be limited memory and recall, which may be limited to fight, flight, search for food and other simple brain functions often viewed as intuition). However, it has not enabled life-forms to morph into other conscious life-forms, as there has not been any survival reason for that to happen. This has allowed life-forms to evolve separately. There is no reason why we would need to be consciously aware of what it is to be like anything else, other than what we are. What purpose would that serve? If there was a competitive edge, evolution would have found it, or perhaps that's for the future?

Trapped in Amber

Trapped in Amber

Be aware of your emotions while reading the narrative.

AN EXPERIMENT THAT CURRENTLY COULD NOT BE DONE, BUT THE POSSIBLE OUTCOMES MAKE FOR AN INTERESTING DEBATE.

Now if we were able to transplant a brain from a woman to a man, who would 'He' become?

The brain is connected to the rest of the body by the spinal cord. However the brain cannot function without the wiring and plumbing in the head. So if a transplant was ever going to be done it would need to include the head of the donor as well. At least that is the current understanding. Now if you can get over the 'yuk' factor and simply consider that this could be done, the question arises, "Who would person 'He' be after the transplant?

I can conceive of four possible answers to this question. Given that my narrative so far is sound in its proposal that the brain is not the resting place of memory, but that all cells of your body play their part in recording and recalling memory, triggered by the environmental signals or thoughts processed by the brain of the life-form.

Possible Outcomes:

1. Even with a new transplanted head and brain from the woman, 'He' would retain his personality and behaviour, including life-style preferences like food, hobbies, habits and phobias, including dress sense.

2. 'He' would become a copy of the woman donor, demonstrating her personality and behaviour, including life-style preferences like food, hobbies, habits and phobias. Possibly even dress sense and make-up.

3. 'He' would be confused. The signals received from 'His' external environment (his senses), would trigger signals in "Her brain' , which is now transplanted on 'His' body, which may not find connections in 'His' memory cells in 'His' body. Or they may find connections that trigger a strange response, and 'He' may not understand his behaviour.

4. 'He' would become a completely new person, with new personality and behaviour, including life-style preferences like food, hobbies, habits and phobias. No memories would be triggered by the external signals entering his new transplanted brain, as there would be no 'software'

connections. Perhaps the process of moving a head from one body to another body would 'wipe' the brain connections, resulting in everything being new again?

Is this exercise a waste of time? I think not, simply because it expands the debate on how the brain, mind, and body connection actually works. Some people will be unable to consider the possible implications of such a make-believe situation. Understand however, your willingness to debate this issue is not only down to intellect, but down to your belief system ... do you think it is worth discussing or not?

Whether you think so or not will depend on your belief system. Your belief system will enable you to participate in those aspects and areas of life that your belief system considers relevant to your beliefs. In a very basic way we are all made from the same atoms, we are all Human Beings; it is only our belief system that marks us out as different people.

Trapped in Amber

Be aware of your emotions while reading the narrative.

CHALLENGING THOUGHTS FOR YOU TO REFLECT UPON.

Wherever there is Truth there is conflict and division. Wherever there is possibility there is probability and change.

Truth implies that there is no alternative; if you say you have the truth, then you are saying that unless others agree with you, they are wrong. This cannot be a basis on which knowledge is built. Truth is stagnant and unmoving; possibilities are what we build with the bricks of truth. Truth is only a tool for us to seek deeper understanding to enable dreams, and potential to unify, and feed the growth of the kaleidoscopic paradigm shift, in life's evolution.

Consider some current knowledge.
The conscious-mind can process forty nerve impulses per second. The sub-conscious-mind can process forty million nerve impulses per second. Each eye has about 1.2 million nerve fibres connected to the brain. The brain can receive signals at four hundred billion bits per second. What does this mean?

It means everything has to be filtered through our conscious-mind because that is the process which allows us to function as humans. The process is deliberately slower than all the other processes (signal receiving abilities of the body). The brain receives four hundred billion bits of information per second from all the many senses of your body. We are only conscious forty times per second, which equates to about two thousand bits per second. Where do the extra 'bits' that the brain receives go? Is it possible that they are filtered through your belief system? Under normal everyday circumstances, if you do not believe it, you will not experience it, even if your brain does.

Your belief system, your behaviour, your memory, your subconscious is what you have taught yourself to be; therefore your brain uses this filter to sort the signals it is receiving, to allow you to operate in the way that you have decided you want to behave. Something traumatic or with no stored similar memory will register in your consciousness, and await a filing instruction (a peptide, an emotion attached to an action), which you have to create. If you do not then you will 'freeze' (stand still); if the situation is really traumatic, and you cannot consciously make a decision, and create a peptide, you will faint. Your body will experience an overload; a part of your operating system will not know what to do, so it will reboot the system (your body). Once rebooted, you may have recall of the event or you may not.

The implication of this is that we cannot possibly perceive the world in our conscious-minds the same way that our brain does. We consciously see what we have been taught to see through the filter of our belief system.

You become what you think about the most.

Your thoughts are not real.

You are creating an illusion and living in it.

According to Sigmund Freud's psychoanalytical theory, the personality is composed of three elements; the ego, Id, and superego. Freud suggested that the Id was present from birth and was driven by the pleasure principle, which strives for immediate gratification of all desires. The ego was the element that is responsible for dealing with reality, while the superego was the aspect of personality that holds all of our internalized moral standards and ideals; our sense of right and wrong. We have moved on since Freud built the foundation for investigation into how the mind works. The 'truth' that he proposed has been tested and analyzed and improved upon with significant advancements in biology and chemistry. As is the case with all knowledge we learn more tomorrow as we build upon what we know today.

Knowledge builds on the shoulders of great men and women who dared to suggest controversial ideas, often with personal cost to themselves.

We identify ourselves through the 'I' and the 'Me' in language. The 'Me' is a concept which includes the body, inferring separateness. Could the 'I' be the observer of our thoughts and images that we mentioned on page 147? Could the 'I' be consciousness?

We tend to operate within two primary concepts; one is cognitive (thinking state) the other is affective (feeling state). Both states have a sense of self. It is the sense of 'me' that allows the facility of other. The 'I' creates the subject from which an object can be discerned.

It is often proposed that adults operate the majority of the time in a cognitive state, while children live in the affective state. Biologists are suggesting that many other life-forms live their entire life in the affective state. Perhaps it is this ability to be influenced by something other than feelings that differentiates humans from other life-forms.

There is no truth only possibilities, and the possibilities suggested by the results of new knowledge is that we do not have an ego, Id or superego. We are not made up of three separate 'things' that form our personality and behaviour. I am proposing that we only work one way, and that is through the influence of genetics and environment. It is recognized that in most cases environment plays a greater role in behavioural outcomes, as environment can, and does have an impact on the genes in the body, whereas the genetic make-up of the individual has little impact in determining the environment, and genetics can be altered by the external environment.

The Ego, Id, and Superego are all replaced by the belief system, and the belief system is a direct product of the external/internal environment (the many senses). We are all controlled by what we believe.

I have included a Spider Diagram showing the results of some of the data I collected randomly from six clients, to evidence the effectiveness of using the techniques and knowledge from this book, after only six sessions.

The diagram clearly shows, that clients who fully participated in the programme of change, made significant enhancements to their health and well-being in a very short period.

Trapped in Amber

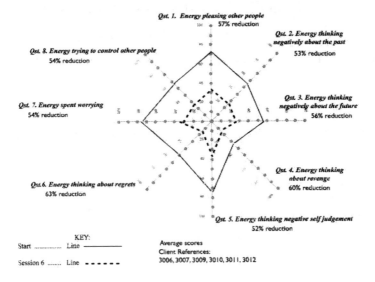

Spider Diagram: The Lucy Theory Psychotherapy Study

Qst. 1. Energy pleasing other people
57% reduction

Qst. 2. Energy thinking negatively about the past
53% reduction

Qst. 8. Energy trying to control other people
54% reduction

Qst. 3. Energy thinking negatively about the future
56% reduction

Qst. 7. Energy spent worrying
54% reduction

Qst. 4. Energy thinking about revenge
60% reduction

Qst. 6. Energy thinking about regrets
63% reduction

Qst. 5. Energy thinking negative self judgement
52% reduction

KEY:
Start .... Line ——————
Session 6 .... Line ▬ ▬ ▬ ▬ ▬

Average scores
Client References:
3006, 3007, 3009, 3010, 3011, 3012

You can significantly enhance your life, by recognising your addiction to your belief system and repeated thoughts, and empowering yourself to change, using the techniques explained in this book.

... you become what you think about the most ...

... your thoughts are not real ...

... you are creating an illusion and living in it ...

Trapped in Amber

Trapped in Amber

Be aware of your emotions while reading the narrative.

HOW DO YOU LIVE YOUR LIFE?

Do you approach each day by mistake? Do you react to situations and events in a random way? Are you trapped by your addictions to how you think? All addictions come from thought; an addiction is not a material 'thing' it is a result of you repeating an action. Nothing makes you become an alcoholic, drug dependent, depressive or stressed, you do it yourself.

Here are some words to possibly describe your view of life:

By chance	Mishap
By mistake	Random
Calamity	Tragedy
Casualty	Unexpected
Disaster	Unintentional
Haphazard	Unplanned
Misfortune	Unwittingly

You are living your life accidentally

Perhaps you approach each day depending upon chance, luck, serendipity or just plain fluke? Do you believe in magic? Well if any of the following words and phrases fit your life-style then perhaps you do.

Chance	Luck
Fluke	Serendipity
Fortuitous	Unintentional
Happening at the same time	Unplanned

You are living your life coincidently

Living life by accident or by coincidence is empowering other people, and events, to dictate your time on Planet Earth. Perhaps you should consider taking control of your experience, in a human form, with descriptive words like;

Arranged	Dreamed
Choice	Meant to
Deliberate	On Purpose
Designed	Planned
Desired	Proposed
Devised	Schemed

Trapped in Amber

Think of the possibilities of living your life intentionally?

When you live under the banner of 'truth' you are living in your belief system, constantly responding to situations through your learned behaviour, forming judgements and opinions that add to your truth. Your belief and faith in what you believe reinforces doubt, fear, insecurity and regrets.

The Lucy Theory Quadrant

Truth	Possibilities
✳ Current belief system. ✳ Responses to situations. ✳ Judgement and opinions.	✳ Continually revise, update, manage & change belief system. ✳ Awareness, openness, & adaptive responses to situations every day. ✳ Freedom from judgement and opinions.
Belief and Faith (self)	**Probabilities**
✳ Doubt. ✳ Fear. ✳ Insecurity. ✳ Regrets.	✳ Meditation. ✳ Controlling negative thinking. ✳ Clarity of purpose. ✳ Secure in self (love).

When you live under the banner of 'possibilities' you learn how to control limiting beliefs resulting in new and different ways of responding to situations. You are no longer a prisoner of your judgements and opinions. Creating possibilities in one's own mind feeds the probability of controlling negative thinking and limited thinking, which in turn, nurtures (or allows) for clarity of purpose, and opens the way to deeper reflection, meditation, and the security of KNOWING one's self. If this is not an act of love then I do not know what is. The beautiful thing about this wonderful process is that it nurtures and feeds.

Understand that a work role that you may undertake should not be identified with self, should not be identified with you. The work role could be done by others. What you do to earn a living is not your job for life. Do not let what you do for a living define who you are. Your *'job for life'* is you. Your 'job' is to create the best 'you' that is possible; given your circumstances and morphogenetic field of influence. When you were born, a direct debit was set up with the Bank of Life. Every day the Bank of Life takes one day from your life; it matters not to the Bank of Life that you choose to get value for the automatic withdrawal from your life account that is entirely up to you. How much do you value one day of your life? Then what are you doing each day to make sure you get value? Other people could do your work role, but only you can live your life.

It matters not that you are disadvantaged by illness or skill; what matters is how you use the 'you' that you have, and your unknown time available on Planet Earth.

Desire to live your life on purpose. What you desire now may change, and you may change your desires at any time; that is your power, and only your power. It is not in the power of anyone else to change your life, only you can do that. I am not talking about material things; I am talking about love and peace for yourself, and all other living things.

You are not under the control of some invisible entity, or governed by some Devine laws that dictate your destiny through other people's judgement of your life on Planet Earth. Whatever has happened to you in the past; abuse, whether physical of sexual, neglect or illness ... what happened, happened. Do not let the negative things that happened in your past be detrimental to your current moment. What matters is this moment NOW ... create your life based on this moment, and walk into your future with love, and peace ... live each moment from this moment with passion.

Your greatest challenge is to know what it is you desire to do with your short time in this life-cycle. Your past does not equal your future.

The world appears to have polarity or duality; a right way, a wrong way; North, South; you, me, love, hate. This presupposes that polarized objects have a basis in reality when in fact they are only conceptualized signposts. Do you have a materialistic or idealistic view of life? Dualism implies a right or a wrong, and defines conflict in choosing one or the other. If you are not going to be part of the solution, then will you be part of the problem? Life is not separated into a dichotomy. This is illusion. You are part of the whole Universe, it is only your belief system that separates and divides. Is there a thinker behind the thought, or is the 'I' consciousness? (Remember that evidence is growing that the whole Universe is conscious.)

If the average person lives for eighty years then that is 4,160 weeks. However, it is not as straight forward as you thinking you have 4,160 weeks to live, because there are 'things' to consider. For example, what do you spend your time doing?

The following table has been compiled using data from a limited survey compiled locally. If you find that one category is different in your life then you will have to adjust another category to make the end total remain at 168 hours, because that is all the hours you will ever have in one week. You cannot save hours to hold them over for another week, and you cannot extend your week by inventing more hours.

Trapped in Amber

Table of Life:

Hours in week:	Weeks in year:	Weeks in avg. Life span (80 years)
168	52	4160

Activity:	Hours/week		Equiv. Weeks	Life Span Wks Left
Start of life				4,160
First 5 years of life nurture/growing			260	3,900
Next 10 years influenced by nurture			520	3,380

15 years to 18 years old you will spend time;

Activity:	Hours/week		Equiv. Weeks	Life Span Wks Left
Sleeping on average	70		65	3,315
Eating	21		20	3,295
In the bathroom	7		7	3,288
Miscellaneous	37		34	3,254
Travelling to/from school	3	(40 wks)	2	3,252
Doing school activities	30	(40 wks)	21	3,231
12 Weeks school holidays			7	3,224
Total Hours in a Week	168			

18 years to 67 years old you will spend time;

Activity:	Hours/week		Equiv. Weeks	Life Span Wks Left
Sleeping on average	60		910	2,314
Eating	14		212	2,102
In the bathroom	8		121	1,981
Miscellaneous	44		667	1,314
At work	35	(48 Wks)	490	824
Travelling to/from work	7	(48 Wks)	98	726
4 weeks per year holiday			50	676
Total Hours in a Week	168			

67 years onwards you will spend time;

Activity:	Hours/week	Equiv. Weeks	Life Span Wks Left
Sleeping on average	40	161	515
Eating	10	40	475
In the bathroom	10	40	435
Miscellaneous	106	427	8
Time shopping	2	8	0
Total Hours in a Week	168		

Miscellaneous activities include preparing food, house work, resting, watching TV, reading, college or further education or investment in learning new skills, and socializing. Special Note: there is no time added for you to be ill.

What this table shows you is;
• In the first fifteen years of life you will probably sleep on average 300 weeks. Add this to the 1,136 weeks average sleep after fifteen years old, and this totals 1,436 weeks. This equates to 35% of your allotted time. So your 4,160 weeks is reduced to 2,724.

• Work and related travel will consume 588 weeks; related to the 2,724 weeks not sleeping, equates to 22% of your waking time allocation. If you took the total weeks sleeping 1,436, plus the work related weeks 588, together they would represent 49% of your allotted time.

• Assuming that in your first fifteen years of life you will eat on average 2 hours per day, this equates to 65 weeks of eating. Add this to the rest of your eating in your life time, and this adds up to 337 weeks. This equates to 12% of your waking time.

• Let us assume that in the first fifteen years of life you spend on average 1.5 hours per day using bathroom facilities (including shower and bath), add this to your other bathroom usage, and the total is 217 weeks. This equates to 8% of your allotted waking time.

Let's reflect on and summarize the above. Take sleep time out of the calculation because you are not active when you are asleep and cannot make changes to your life. This means that if you lived for eighty years you would have 2,724 weeks of waking time; 22% of that time is spent on work related issues.

How many of you actually love what you do for a living? How many of you actually desire to do the work that you are doing? Well, if the answer to the above is 'no', then you are wasting 22% of your waking life. What are you doing it for, and more important what are you going to do about it?

If you give the usual excuses regarding money, lack of opportunity, lack of skills, and other similar excuses, then reflect on this question. Who is responsible for your life?

Clearly the Table of Life above does not represent your life. It is a table constructed from limited data to prompt a question, and that is; 'Do you know what you are doing with the time that's available to you?'

I have constructed Exercise 5 below for you to complete. Understand that you have only got 168 hours in one week. It is not possible to have more or less, you can not carry any hours over into the next week, nor can you use hours from the future. Once your time has gone ... it has gone. I have listed some activities that are fairly common. If you have other activities in your life then there is space for you to add those. Follow the formula given, and discover your Table of Life. From this information you can then start to realise where you will find the time to make the worthwhile changes you desire. There is no value in doing the exercise in relation to the past, as your past does not equal your future. What has gone has gone, focus on this moment, for it is this moment only that you will make your first step of change. The start of every journey begins in the mind, the action begins in the moment.

Your body is finite, your impact on the Universe is infinite, for you are the Universe. Energy cannot be destroyed; it can only be changed from one form into another, so states the first law of thermodynamics, namely the conservation of energy. Your life cannot be destroyed, only changed. The second law of thermodynamics states that entropy of an isolated System always increases; in other words. If the time for changing your life is not now, then when?

Trapped in Amber

Exercise 5: Individual Table of Life

Hours in week: *Weeks in year:*   *Weeks in avg. Life span (80 years)*
    168   *52*   *4160*

What age will you be on your next birthday? Write that number down and take it away from 67. (67 years is the average age when people will retire from work. This may change, if it does then use the new retirement age.)

You have now calculated the number of years you have to go until you reach the age of 67 years old. Multiply your answer by 52 and this will show you how many weeks that will be.

Fill in the column 'A' in the following table and then do the calculations

Trapped in Amber

How much time in hours do you spend each week on the following activities?

Activity	COLUMN A How many hours per week do you spend doing the activity?	COLUMN B Divide column A by 168 and then multiply by 100 to get percentage. %
Sleeping		
Bathroom / bath/ shower/ teeth/ toilet		
Shopping		
Preparing food		
Eating		
Travel work/college		
Work/college including time at home with reading and homework etc.		
Watching TV/playing computer games.		
Reading for pleasure or knowledge not connected with work / college		
The Total	168	

Trapped in Amber

I have left some blank spaces for you to fill in activities specific to your life-style. The more you can identify specific activities the greater opportunity for change. Remember the total number of hours you spend each week on activities MUST TOTAL 168 hours; if your total is less than 168 hours, then add a column called miscellaneous, until you can identify the activity(s) that are taking your time up each week.

Divide the number of hours spent on each activity by 168 (the number of hours in a week). Then multiply your answer by 100 to show the percentage time for each activity.

With this information you can now appreciate the impact of each activity on your life.

Above you calculated the number of weeks you have to live until you retire. From the data you have collected in Column B, you could calculate the number of weeks you will spend until you retire, doing each activity in the list.

Many people often complain that they do not have enough hours in the week to do the things they *'desire to do'*. I have often found that when they do this exercise they often go into denial mode. It is as if they would rather believe they have not got enough hours in the week, rather than have the knowledge that they have.

Trapped in Amber

Trapped in Amber

... you have all the time there is, and your life is the product of your choices ...

... other people could do your work role, but only you can live your life ...

Trapped in Amber

Trapped in Amber

Be aware of your emotions while reading the narrative.

IS IT POSSIBLE?

The following is a new and personal theory; I ask you to read the narrative without judgement. If you find yourself disagreeing or agreeing with the theory then please move that thought. Remember that forming an opinion or judgement limits your ability, as it confines your thinking into a predetermined space of right or wrong, black or white. If you must assume a stance then use the neutral thought of *'interesting'* as the hook for your feelings. Let the words sink into your sub-conscious, and leave them there under the heading of interesting. Then as you go through life, events will happen that will allow you to test out the theory for yourself. You will then form your own view on the subject. Please remember I do not desire you to believe anything ... I desire you to know it.

When we move into silence we allow ourselves to be present in the moment, and in that moment is the connection to our source. Now religious minded people would suggest that silence brings you closer to 'God'. There is no proof whatsoever for this statement, it is based on thinking from two thousand years ago when knowledge of how the world worked, and how humans worked, was inaccurate and controlled by the Church. Silence is not the property of religion; it is not a doorway to a Divinity, it is the Universal right of all life-forms, and a path leading us to reflection, by connecting us all to the one living matrix, the Universe; the source from which everything comes. Is it possible that we are not made by a 'Divine Being'? Could it be probable that we are, and always shall be, part of the fabric of the Universe? Perhaps there is no need to worship or honor that source, only to respect and love all life-forms because we are literally one. Perhaps there is no separation. Could it be that we have to take responsibility for the form we are in, not pretend we are controlled? These are not statements; they are questions for you to answer.

Could it have been the case that claims of a 'God' were the response to questions that the leaders of the day had no answer to, so they invented the concept of a God that gave them power and thus control? Is it possible that God is an answer to justify power and control, and perhaps it has no basis in knowledge, only belief? Again these are not statements, they are questions for you to answer.

I am not suggesting there is no God, and I am not suggesting there is; I am asking questions that should be answered after rigorous experimentation and observation, not hooked to a belief that we have no real knowledge or experience of. Could it be that the old adage, that God's word should not be questioned, only confirms man's need to hold onto power through ignorance?

There is strong evidence that we do not work by magic, we are made of atoms, all of which were made in the formation and destruction of stars. Everything, including the Planet Earth is made from the atoms created from stars. The Universe is made up of atoms. We are all intimately connected to the Universe. So I would like to propose something so controversial that most belief systems will initially think it is ridiculous. Hold on you've come this far. Some of the narrative has been unconventional, but the techniques work ... don't they? I know they do. So here goes, are you ready?

You know current scientific, empirical, and verifiable knowledge suggests that we are made from atoms, and that those atoms make cells, which make organs, which make living entities. This is the best guess or understanding that our accepted knowledge at this moment agrees upon. It is accepted that within the cell there are organelles. These are organs within cells. In the eukaryotic cell, the organelles are the anatomy systems of the cell. The organelles are alive, therefore there must be an experience as, or life as, an organelle'. A cell is alive. If it is alive then there must be an experience as 'the life of a cell'. An atom is alive, or at least it vibrates, and moves, and is present in everything; so we could say that there must be an experience as 'life as an atom'. Just because we cannot experience the organelle, cell or atom 'life', does not mean that they are not as real as the experience you call 'life'.

There are more micro-organisms in your body than there are cells. Trillions of micro-flora bacteria live in the human digestive system; they form over one kilogram of your body weight. They are alive and without them we could not exist. They break down the food remains that have been digested, and they stop harmful bacteria and fungus from invading the body. These 'gut' bacteria also produce vitamin K, which is essential for normal blood clotting.

Living microbes inhabit every surface of a healthy adult human that is exposed or accessible from the outside. It is estimated that fifty million individual bacteria live on a square centimeter of skin surface of our bodies. Imagine the crowds of people shopping in all the major stores in a large city the day before Christmas ... well that is what one square centimeter of your skin looks like all the time. It is suggested that more than half of our body weight consists of foreign micro-organisms; more than one hundred and fifteen different species live on our skin alone. Microorganisms exist in every cell; without them the cell would die ... and so would we.

What I am suggesting is that there are many different ways of looking at 'life' as a concept. There is the 'life' of an ant, elephant, dog, cat, fly; there is the 'life' as a tree, or plant; there is the 'life' as bacteria, and algae. We only tend to look at life from a perspective of 'the global self' or other life-forms that we can see. I would suggest that the majority of people do not think of an atom as having a life?

Now that suggestion hopefully would have made you reflect on how small an atom is compared to say ... an average human adult. An atom is having a 'life' inside an organelle, inside a cell, inside an organ, inside a life-form.

Are you sitting down in a safe place because here come the crazy idea? Is it possible that the Universe is a life-form, and Planet Earth is a cell in that life-form, and the life-forms on Planet Earth are some of the organelles of the Earth Cell? If some of the organelles in the Earth Cell are human-kind, then the behaviour of any cell will totally depend upon its parts and will behave accordingly. Therefore if the Mankind-organelle infuses insecurity, fear, and doubt (with the corresponding actions) into the Earth Cell, then the cell's behaviour will be infected with the man-made disease of greed, and hate. Then like all diseased cells, it will either perish, or with the help of the other organelles (on the Earth Cell) it will form an attack and destroy the disease.

The life-entity, the Universe, will not suffer for the deeds of one cell. That Earth Cell will either heal itself or it will perish. The Universe demands unity within its fundamental laws. It is possible, and strong rigorous evidence exists to demonstrate, that it is probable that life is not a product of a Divine God, but part of the conditions of a living Universe.

Today will soon be tomorrow, when it will become yesterday; you know what you did yesterday, so if you don't change today, then your tomorrow (future) will be the same.

Is it possible that we see life as a sequential series of events? Events that either involve us personally or events that affect others. It seems that we put meaning and value to these aspects of our life. Perhaps more meaning is attributed to those events that have a personal connection to us, than those events which appear to be distant and affecting only strangers, far removed from our 'sphere' of influence. Yet we can choose, and often do, to be selective in what we attribute meaning. This human trait seems to confirm to us that we are separate, and that we have the ability of interpreting events in line with our belief system, reinforcing or influencing our view of 'life'.

Is it not strange, that often others are in disagreement with your interpretation and values. How can that be when they experienced that same event as you?

Have you ever asked the question why we see personal events as an adjective to describe our own life?

Is it possible that if we accept that we are atoms, and therefore part of the Universe, then we must be part of Planet Earth? If we are part of Planet Earth then all events on Planet Earth make up life? If we can only experience a very small part of all the events on the Planet, then how can we possibly say we understand what life is?

Could it be that we only understand, within the boundaries of the meanings and values we have attached to known events, and that those meanings, and values have forged our belief system? If that is so, then how do we know our interpretation of the event is correct? Where did we get the rules from that empowered us to have the right understanding? And how come people differ so much in their understanding of the same event?

Clearly, understanding is not a Universal rule, in that everyone would have the same understanding if they experienced the same event. So understanding must be a condition and product of the individual belief system.

We gain our emotional values from our environment ... our senses. We only interpret what we are aware of ... we cannot, without reflection and contemplation, be aware of what we are not aware. How do you know what you do not know?

What strategy do you employ?

- Ignore what it is you don't know, because you are all right without it? Is this not delusion? How do you know you could not be better?
- Set-up a belief, accepting the world works by magic or under the control of some Devine Entity? Is this not delusion? Why don't all people with 'A Belief in a Devine Entity' live in peace, harmony, health and love? Your justification to answer this question is only a product of your belief system ... your belief system is not real, you have made it up, and there is rigorous evidence all around you to demonstrate this.
- Do you desire to know and understand that which is possible in this moment to understand?

If you could consider that you are part of a whole, and not separate, and that your body form was a vessel for '*you*' to experience life on Planet Earth; then is it possible for '*you*' to acknowledge that '*you*' must be the controller, of that body form? Therefore if '*you*' are the controller, any abilities of the body form are only limited by '*your*' belief.

Perhaps the reader has noticed I have put '*you*' in emphasized italics. This is implying that '*you*' are not your body. '*You*' are in your body, but not of the body. Is that possible?

If your initial body form was different from the general population when you were born, or has developed a health issue since birth, then you have that health issue to deal with. How you deal with that issue is entirely your responsibility. You are born with what you are born with, or, perhaps through no fault of your own, you develop a body issue affecting your health; that is what you have to live your life. What are you going to do?

If you are an adult, and you were born with no health issues, but now you have, is it possible that you have been instrumental in that process? The choices you have made have brought you to where you are; you could not be in the place you are unless you had travelled there yourself.

Take responsibility, and don't blame anyone or anything for where you find yourself, for this moment cannot be altered by thinking about what happened. The past does not equal your future. Is it possible, that if you made different choices in this moment, and continued to make different choices from your past choices in the moments to come, you could be somewhere else?

Do you like being a victim?
Are you comfortable with what you believe?
Are you frightened of change?

Trapped in Amber

Let me propose an interesting question that will demonstrate the difference between believing and knowing ... the difference between belief and knowledge.

Question:
Do you believe that you are going to die or do you know it?

Do you understand the difference between belief and knowing now? It would seem that the human condition of ignoring knowledge that they either feel is not relevant at a particular moment or is just too uncomfortable to think about, can be dismissed and accepted as a belief. People consider that it is a belief that some day they will die. There is strong empirical evidence that we will without any doubt all die, do you agree? It would appear that people hide behind a belief rather than take responsibility. Could it be that believing you will die, somehow gives you permission, or provides you with a convenient excuse, for devaluing the experience of your life on Planet Earth?

When you truly accept the knowledge that you will die, don't you then have to take responsibility to contribute to the health and well-being of the Planet as you are only a guest here. Your stay here is temporary. Why do so many waste time abusing their minds and bodies? Time is only a concept; it is not a real thing. Even so, time seems to have an 'arrow' which only goes in one direction. Events are not observed going backwards. The human life span is not even a blink of an eye in the Universe's consciousness. The human life-form will go the same way of all other life-forms that have over exploited their environment. They will be replaced. We should not be worried about saving the Planet for that is not in danger, we should be worried about saving the human life-form for it's time is limited.

Why do we see everything as separate? Nothing divides as much as belief. Belief will hold you within boundaries, fear, doubt, insecurity and regret. Knowledge will empower you to experience this moment, for this moment is all you have until you have the next, and the next moment is a product of the moment before. And so it will be, until you have your last moment in the body form.

Stop believing who you were, start knowing who you are.

Do not live your life trapped in the amber of your belief system; trapped in the amber of what other people have said or done; trapped in the amber of blame and what if. Know that the only judgement made on your life comes from you; it is your gift alone as it is your life.

You do not live on Planet Earth ... you are Planet Earth.
Break free from the amber that entraps your mind and

Love UnConditionally.

Trapped in Amber

Trapped in Amber

A FABLE ABOUT BELIEF AND KNOWLEDGE.

By Gordon F Gatiss

The old teacher sat on a large rock and dangled his feet close to the water flowing below. His eyes were shut and he was counting aloud. "Eight ... nine."

The student approached and coughed.

"Ten." He opened his eyes, and without looking at the student he smiled, and nodded his head slightly.

"Why are you counting Master?"

"I am counting the different noises that the river is making on its journey to the sea."

The student glanced at the river, and heard only the sound of the flowing water. He coughed again nervously ... "Master I want to understand the difference between belief and knowledge. Can you tell me?"

The sounds from the river wove through the mind of the Teacher as he stared lovingly at the sixteen shapes he could see that created the movement in the water. Without deflecting his gaze the Teacher said, "Choose a stone from the river bank."

The student walked around the embankment looking at the stones, which were all shapes and sizes. "How big should the stone be?"

"Your choice."

The student kicked a few stones, rolling them over, and then he spotted a stone with red veins of iron running through it. He felt that this was the one, and he bent down to pick it up. It weighted around ten kilos, so two hands were needed as he carried it back to his Teacher. Without looking up the Teacher said, "Carry the stone everywhere you go for the next seven days." The Teacher raised his hand, and the student understood his time in conversation was over.

Everyone the student came into contact with asked the question, "Why are you carrying that stone around with you?" His reply was always the same, "I am understanding the difference between belief and knowledge."

Then one person asked. "How is carrying a stone around with you going to teach you the difference between belief and knowledge?"

The student looked puzzled and replied, "I believe it will become clear in seven days ... the Masters has set me this task."

The days passed, and the stone seemed to get heavier. The student made a sling, which he hung around his neck to hold the stone so it was easier to carry. During the seven days the student became weary of carrying the stone. It was a burden when he wanted to play games with the other students. He would take it to every meal, to the bathroom, to lessons, when he went for a walk, and he even took it to bed with him. At the end of seven days he went looking for his Master, again finding him sitting by the river, he approached him, and coughed gently.

Without looking up the Master said, "Well have you understood the difference?"

There was silence as the student pondered the question. "I do not understand Master I have done what you asked, but I have not discovered the answer."

"What have you done?"

"I have carried this stone around with me for seven days."

"Why?"

"Because you told me to."

"Why?"

"Because I asked you to tell me the difference between belief and knowledge."

"So have you understood?"

There was a long silence before he replied. "No Master."

"Tell me what you did from the very beginning."

"Well I wanted to understand the difference between belief and knowledge, and you told me to pick a stone and ..."

"Did I tell you which stone to pick?"

"No ... I made the choice ... then you told me to carry it around with me for seven days."

"Why?"

The student looked puzzled, but after a short silence he smiled and nodded. "I believed that after seven days I would understand the difference between belief and knowledge."

"And do you?"

"No."

"So will you continue to carry the stone?"

He hesitated, "If you feel I should Master."

"What do you feel?"

"I would prefer to understand."

"Then understand that you chose to carry the stone as part of your belief that there was an outcome. I did not make you ... it was your choice. No one can make you believe anything; you have to do that yourself. Every belief that is carried with an outcome attached, is like that stone ... it has weight, and will limit your potential. Belief entraps you in repeated behaviour, specializing in thought, with limited alternatives. You do not carry knowledge, for knowledge walks silently beside you, guiding, teaching, protecting, and empowering responsibility. Belief has emotional triggers, knowledge is not an option, it is a practice that empowers choice and responsibility. Now go and decide if you want to live your life under a banner of faith and belief, or knowledge."

With that the Teacher raised his hand, closing his eyes in meditation.

'Plop, gurgle, slush, ting, burp', the sounds came from the river ... the student stared wide-eyed, as his mouth fell open. Reflection can often leave the 'observer' open to emotional confusion and restlessness.

Gordon

A SPIRITUAL REVOLUTION

On the surface of the world right now there is war, violence, and things
seem dark.
But calmly and quietly, at the same time,
something else is happening underground.
An inner revolution is taking place,
and certain individuals are being called to a higher light.
It is a silent revolution. From the inside out. From the ground up.
This is a Global operation. A Spiritual Conspiracy.
There are sleeper cells in every nation on the planet.
You won't see us on TV.
You won't read about us in the newspaper.
You won't hear about us on the radio.
We don't seek any glory. We don't wear any uniform.
We come in all shapes and sizes, colors and styles.
Most of us work anonymously.
We are quietly working behind the scenes,
in every country, and culture of the world.
Cities big and small, mountains and valleys,
in farms and villages, tribes and remote islands.
You could pass by one of us on the street, and not even notice.
We go undercover. We remain behind the scenes.
It is of no concern to us who takes the final credit,
but simply that the work gets done.
Occasionally we spot each other in the street;
we give a quiet nod and continue on our way.
During the day many of us pretend we have normal jobs,
but behind the false storefront at night is where the real work takes
place.
Some call us the Conscious Army.
We are slowly creating a new world,
with the power of our minds and hearts.

Trapped in Amber

We follow, with passion and joy.

Our orders come from the Central Spiritual Intelligence

We are dropping soft, secret love bombs when no one is looking

Poems ~ Hugs ~ Music ~ Photography ~ Movies ~ Kind words ~

Smiles ~ Meditation and prayer ~ Dance ~ Social activism ~ Websites

Blogs ~ Random acts of kindness.

We each express ourselves in our own unique ways with our own

unique gifts and talents.

Be the change you want to see in the world.

That is the motto that fills our hearts.

We know it is the only way real transformation takes place.

We know that quietly and humbly we have the

power of all the oceans combined.

Our work is slow and meticulous like the formation of mountains.

It is not even visible at first glance, and yet with it entire tectonic plates

shall be moved in the centuries to come.

Love is the new religion of the 21st century.

You don't have to be a highly educated person,

or have any exceptional knowledge to understand it.

It comes from the intelligence of the heart, embedded in the timeless

evolutionary pulse of all human beings.

Be the change you want to see in the world.

Nobody else can do it for you.

We are now recruiting.

Perhaps you will join us, or already have.

All are welcome - The door is open.

Author unknown

Do I Know Nothing Anymore   (Copyright Nigel Gatiss)

Do I know nothing anymore?
Or am I all knowledge and understanding
That my wisdom is, but the wisdom of the last book?
Do I ingest its contents, feed my soul,
And feel nourished by the words?
Do they cast a spell that makes peace of war, Heaven from Hell?
Is it '*I*' or '*Is,*' that cast what shade of grey or black today,
'That thinks not?'
Do I retain my freedom?
Or does doctrine close the door
If I am not moulded like clay, and filed away?
Do I believe to deceive,
And become a follower once more?
For is there not comfort in the crowd?
Am I afraid to shout too loud,
Reach beyond my teacher's door,
And just accept what's gone before,
Because it is … '*The Universal Law?*'
But then… 'I know nothing anymore.'

Trapped in Amber

Moments   (Copyright Nigel Gatiss)

Once again, the days are flowing silently on.

How soon each fleeting second is spent,

And filed away in the realms of memory.

I want to grasp each moment,

Caress it in my hands,

For the precious creation it is.

'Time,' conceived from the void:

For in reality, can there ever be, in time, a future?

Is it a creation of imagination?

Something mystic, mysterious,

And a magic beyond belief.

If I try to comprehend its construction, its form,

I become, absorbed, spellbound,

For it is beyond my understanding.

The moment is - NOW!

And as I let it slip through my trembling fingers,

Did I touch it with love?

A tear falls upon the page.

The salt stained pool, denies the pen, to break the spell, and bring
me back to reality, once again.

Trapped in Amber

Consciousness   (Copyright Nigel Gatiss)

Born amongst the stars:
A journey remembered well.
Although I appear to exist on this beautiful world,
This soul is just a visitor here,
Longing;
Like all lost souls,
For the familiar comforts of its birth,
Ashes to stardust -
A returning home.

Trapped in Amber

It's (The Purpose of Life)   (Copyright Gordon F Gatiss)

It's the swaying branches in the unseen breeze,
The drop of water that feeds the trees.
The fragrant perfume of the coloured flowers,
The shadows at night - the seas great powers.
The child's smile an eye with a tear,
A waterfall ... a glass window that's clear.
The gift of sight to those who are blind,
A gift of discovery to those who can find.
It's a gentle touch a hard word or two,
Loosing ones temper, the thought of you.
It's the noise of a car, sight of the moon;
The end of a moment coming too soon.
It's sitting alone by a cosy fire,
Climbing a mountain, going higher and higher.
Opening a door let a stranger inside,
Touching a leaf in the countryside.
A dinner a breakfast – it's any meal,
Reflections in mirrors, thoughts that appeal.
It can cross water, land, air or time,
Can lean forward or recline.
It can be a seed or a towering oak,
A spider, an insect, a laugh or a joke.
It can be tender with feeling, long lasting or short,
But unlike a ball it cannot be caught.
It's a game of chance like throwing a dice,
Hot or cold, awful or nice.
It's educational, an experience, a growing tool,
It can be good or bad or look like a fool.
It's hard and it's soft, it can not be seen,
You can touch it and feel it, so it's not just a dream.
If planted carefully and tendered with care,
Honesty and truthfulness they will grow there.
You can take it away, you can stop it from living;
You can not stop it from being or stop it being given.
It's a hundred and one things, below and above,
Four little words describe it, **Peace, Forgiveness and Love**.

Trapped in Amber

The question was "How?"

The answer came, "If you can see the possibility then you create the probability, and the Universe will do the rest."

Trapped in Amber

Trapped in Amber

A good scientific model or theory is underlined by simple accepted rules.

1. The theory is elegant. It does not rely on magic; it uses current knowledge (limited as that might be) with new interpretations of that knowledge, to build an explanation to an unanswered question.
2. It contains few arbitrary or adjustable elements. It uses as much current accepted knowledge, or the best guess or understanding available, with perhaps one step-change in thinking.
3. It agrees with and explains all existing observations.
4. Makes detailed predictions about future observations that can be disproved or falsify the theory if they (the predictions) are not borne out.

What science does demand of a theory is that it is testable.

My explanations of behaviour, belief system and the six steps of how to change your life, plus the shared knowledge on consciousness, qualia, and why can we not be consciously aware of what it is like to be someone else, adhere to all the above criteria. My challenge to you is to test it for yourself, remember your refusal is only a product of your belief system.

Trapped in Amber

Trapped in Amber

SOURCES OF INFORMATION

- Anda RF, Croft JB, Felitti VJ, Nordenberg D, Giles WH, Williamson DF, Giovino GA. Adverse childhood experiences and smoking during adolescence and adulthood. Journal of the American Medical Association. 1999; 282:1652-1658.

- Anda RF, Felitti VJ, Chapman DP, Croft JB, et al. Abused boys, battered mothers, and male involvement in teen pregnancy: New insights for pediatricians. Pediatrics 2001: 107(2), e19.

- Anda RF, Whitfield CL, Felitti VJ, Chapman D, Edwards VJ, Dube SR, Williamson DF. Alcohol-impaired parents and adverse childhood experiences: the risk of depression and alcoholism during adulthood. Journal of Psychiatric Services 2002; 53(8):1001-1009.

- BBC 4 documentary with Jim Al-Khalili, Everything and Nothing, March 2011.

- Burr, H. (1972), 'The Fields of Life': New York: Ballantine

- Cohen, J M. (2007) 'Reconnecting with Nature': Ecopress.

- Cox, B. (Prof) & Cohen, A, 'Wonders of the Universe': Harper Collins Publishers.

- Dawkins, R. (1989), 'The Selfish Gene': 2nd edition, Oxford: Oxford University Press

- Dietz PM, Spitz AM, Anda RF, Williamson DF, McMahon PM, Santelli JS, Nordenberg DF, Felitti VJ, Kendrick JS. Unintended pregnancy among adult women exposed to abuse or household dysfunction during their childhood. Journal of the American Medical Association. 1999;282:1359-1364.

- Dirac, P. (2003) 'Lectures on Quantum Mechanics': Dover Publications.

- Dong M, Anda RF, Felitti VJ, Dube SR, Giles WH. The Relationship of Exposure to Childhood Sexual Abuse to Other Forms of Abuse, Neglect and Household Dysfunction during Childhood. (In press, Child Abuse and Neglect).

- Dube SR, Anda RF, Felitti VJ, Chapman D, Williamson DF, Giles WH. Childhood abuse, household dysfunction and the risk of attempted suicide throughout the life span: Findings from Adverse Childhood Experiences Study. Journal of the American Medical Association. 2001: 286, 3089-3096.

- Dube SR, Anda RF, Felitti VJ, Chapman DP, Giles WH. Childhood Abuse, Neglect and Household Dysfunction and the Risk of Illicit Drug Use: The Adverse Childhood Experience Study. Pediatrics 2003; 111(3): 564-572.

- Dube SR, Anda RF, Felitti VJ, Edwards VJ, Croft JB. (2002). Adverse Childhood Experiences and personal alcohol abuse as an adult. Addictive Behaviors, 2002. 27(5), 713-725.

- Eden, D. (1998), Energy Medicine': Piatkus Books Ltd.

- Emoto, M. (2004), 'The Hidden Messages in Water': Oregon USA, Beyond Words Publishing.

- Felitti VJ, Anda RF, Nordenberg D, Williamson DF, Spitz AM, Edwards V, Koss MP, et al JS. 'The relationship of adult health status to childhood abuse and household dysfunction': American Journal of Preventive Medicine. 1998; 14:245-258.

- Finlay, BL, Darlington, RB, & Nicastro, N. (2001) 'Developmental structure in brain evolution': *Behavioral and Brain Sciences* 24 (2): XXX-XXX.

- Frohlich, H. (1968), 'Long range coherence and energy storage in biological systems': International Journal of Quantum Chemistry, 2: 641-649

- Goswami, A. (1995), 'The Self-Aware Universe: How Consciousness Creates the Material World': Jeremy P Tarcher

- Gribbin, J. (2000), 'Stardust': Penguin Group

- Hartmann, T. (1998), 'The Last Hours of Ancient Sunlight': Mythical Books

- Hawking, S. (2001), 'The Universe in a Nutshell': Bantam

- Hawkings, S. Mlodinow, L. (2010), 'The Grand Design': Bantam Press

- Heisenberg, W. (2003),Physical Principles of the Quantum Theory: Translated by Carl Eckhart & F.C. Hoyt: Dover Publications.

- Hillis SD, Anda RF, Felitti VJ, Nordenberg D, Marchbanks PA. Adverse childhood experiences and sexually transmitted diseases in men and women: a retrospective study. Pediatrics 2000 106(1):E11.

- Jastrow, R. (1981), 'The Enchanted Loom, Mind in the Universe': Simon Schuster

- Jaynes, J. (1982), 'The Origin of Consciousness in the Breakdown of the Bicameral Mind: Houghton Mifflin

- Kerouak, J. (2000), 'On the Road': Longman

- Lipton, B. (2005), 'The Biology of Belief': Llandeilo: Cygnus Books

- Lipton, H Bruce. Bhaerman, S. (2009) 'Spontaneous Evolution': Hay House

- Margulis, L. (1998), 'Five Kingdoms: An Illustrated Guide to the Phyla of Life on Earth', 3rd Edition: W H Freeman Publishers

- McTaggart, L. (2003), 'The Field': Harper Collins,

- National Library of Poetry (1994), 'Dance on the Horizon': Watermark Press

- Norretranders, T (1999): ' The User Illusion': Penguin Books

Trapped in Amber

- Penrose, R. (1995), 'Shadows of the mind': Vintage London

- Penrose, R. (1999), 'The Emperor's New Mind': Oxford University Press

- Penrose, R. (2010), 'Cycles of Time': The Bodley Head

- Pert, C. (1997), 'Molecules of Emotion – Why you feel the way you feel': Simon & Schuster

- Plimmer, M. & King, B. (2004), 'Beyond Coincidence': Icon Books

- Popp, F. A., Gu, Qiao and Li, Ke-Hsueh (1994), 'Biophoton emission: experimental background and theoretical approaches': Modern Physics Letters B, 8 (21/22): 1269-96

- Radin, D. (1997), 'The Conscious Universe': Harper Collins Publishers

- Radin, D. (2006), 'Entangled Minds': Pocket Books

- Revolver Entertainment, (2006), 'What the Bleep – Down the Rabbit Hole': DVD

- Seth, AK. Izhilkevich, E. Reeke, GN. And Edelman GM. 'Proceedings of the National Academy of Science', July 11th 2006, Vol. 103: 10799-10804

- Sheldrake, R. (1987), 'A New Science of Life': London: Paladin

- Sheldrake, R. (2005)

- Talbot, M. (1991), 'The Holographic Universe': Grafton Books

- Tiller, W.A. (1997), 'Science of Human Transformation': Pavior Publishing

- Tiller, W.A. Dibble, W. Kohane, M. (2001), 'Conscious Acts of Creation': Pavior Publishing

- Tolle, E. (1999), 'The Power of Now': New World Library

Trapped in Amber